D1433219

FOOTBALL LEXICON

FOOTBALL LEXICON

LEIGH & WOODHOUSE

faber and faber

In association with The Oleander Press

First published in 2004 by The Oleander Press
This edition first published in 2004
in association with The Oleander Press
by Faber and Faber Limited
3 Queen Square, London, WC1N 3AU

Printed in England by Mackays

A CIP catalogue record for this book is available
from the British Library.

0–571–22797–X

2 4 6 8 10 9 7 5 3 1

Preface

Football fans don't only watch football. They talk it. They listen to it. They need to read and hear all about it. A whole industry, ranging from match commentaries and the sports pages of newspapers to radio phone-ins and websites, caters for this need every day of the week.

It has not always been thus. Originally, the task of football commentators and reporters was that of conveying information for the benefit of those not present at a match. There was indeed once a fear that people might be deterred from going to a match if they knew it had been selected for live radio commentary. Hence the practice (which now looks quaint and self-important) of not disclosing the location of the honoured venue before kick-off. And even then the commentator might reveal it in a tantalisingly protracted way: 'To my right, I see lights coming on in the flats and a wisp of smoke from a distant chimney, while a flag flutters aloft on the stand opposite: yes, of course, we're at the Dell for Southampton v Everton'.

This scruple was abandoned, not because it no longer seemed that radio commentary could emulate the actual experience of a match, but probably because

it was recognised that they could be complementary.
Some fans indeed go to matches with headphones so
they get both. But the shift indicates a more general
sense that football commentary and reporting do
more than meet the modest task of just providing
information. They provide pleasures and fulfil needs
which are more mysterious. Many fans rush from a
game they have just seen to hear it reported on the
radio, before buying a paper to read about it. Rarely is
it information they want. Instead, it seems, they wish
to see what the match which they have just experienced fleetingly, subjectively and intensely looks like
in the words of someone else.

Television coverage of football, which, like radio
commentary, was greeted with suspicion when it
arrived, has also contributed to changing the nature
of football reporting. It is now likely that many of
those reading a report in a Sunday paper will have
already seen on television, if not actually in the
stadium, some of the action being described. Yet, if
anything, this has liberated reporters from the more
humble task of providing information to concentrate
rather on description and discussion.

Moreover, now that players carry names on their
shirts, cameramen can zoom in and out and we can
activate buttons which provide statistics, you might
have thought that television could dispense with
commentators altogether, since we do not need them
for information. Yet, in common with their counterparts working for newspapers, the jobs of television
commentators have not been threatened but made
more interesting by these changes. Running commentary has become so integral to our experience of
football that you may hear children who are kicking
a ball about in backstreets and schoolyards actually
supply their own commentary as they dribble, shoot
and foul, while computer games which simulate football matches, even as they indulge the fantasy that

you are a Premiership footballer, sometimes provide a commentary in the language of your choice. For all the talk of a visual age, television coverage has made the experience of football even more verbal.

As coverage of football has spread from newspapers to radio and television, a morphology in the language with which it is described may be charted. All sports have their own jargon, their own linguistic idiosyncrasies. The language of football perhaps deserves especial attention. Firstly, of all sports, football seems to arouse in those who watch it the blindest loves and the bitterest hatreds. We watch our team with blinkers. Football commentators and reporters are by and large scrupulous in not allowing themselves to be infected in such a way, but most of them must suppress these emotions rather than just not have them. It follows that their language can be heavily euphemistic and also awkwardly hyperbolic on occasions. Secondly, the sheer quantity of matches covered, the pace at which football is played, and the remarkable speed with which journalists have to compile their reports, all necessitate a certain formulaic quality in responses to football. It is sometimes too easy to deplore as clichés the many phrases and words that can act as useful shorthand for the reader or listener. But while football matches are iterative and contain certain invariable situations, one match perhaps differs from another more than in any other sport. The language of commentators and reporters is restless and inventive too, as football matches and football itself take unpredictable turns.

But perhaps the most noticeable phenomenon has been the relatively recent discovery of the talking footballer or talking football manager. Interviews pre- and post-match have introduced us to a new vocabulary.

There was a time when footballers were working-class heroes who earned working-class wages. They might have lived down your street. Yet, unless they did so, they were to football supporters mute figures intermittently visible over a sea of clothcaps. Most people never heard them talk about a match, let alone read their opinions. Then footballers started to move in a different orbit from most of us. But, just as they have disappeared behind tinted windows and electronic gates, they have become more familiar to us than ever, through written and oral interviews. The contrast between the facility with which some stars express themselves on the pitch and their inarticulacy off it can be a source of embarrassment. Language to these footballers is like tarmac to their studs. But the contrast may also be a source of consolation. To an extent, laughter at the way they speak is the revenge of fans on the players they'd love to have been. The clichés and set phrases – sick as a parrot, over the moon, game of two halves – to which players and managers seem to turn at every juncture have indeed been echoed so gleefully and frequently by the public that the mockery of these commonplaces has itself become commonplace. Besides, the language of football players and managers has moved on. You will not hear these phrases at all these days, unless they come coated in irony. Other equally ossified terms may have taken their place, but in general a greater self-consciousness is to be found when players and managers speak. This may stem from the increased prominence of non-native speakers who, in some cases, are making English football discourse more improvised and eccentric, and, in other instances, are rendering it more deliberate and precise, the subset of a language that has actually been learned. At all events, clichés feature less commonly in their parlance. But the increased self-consciousness and variety of expression result more probably from the acknowledged fact that speaking to the press and handling the media are, if you will pardon the cliché, part and parcel of the modern game.

Footballers and their managers continue to be derided for clichés they no longer actually use. We do not intend to add to or update these catalogues, but to identify more pervasive usages, some admirably economic, others less felicitous, in an attempt to circumscribe the changing vocabulary of commentators and reporters as well as the discourse of footballers, to snapshot the contemporary mannerisms of the BBC and *The Times* as well as Robbie Fowler's modern English usage.

A

Academic: Of no import, of no consequence whatsoever. Likely to appeal chiefly, or only, to pedants: 'The Slovenia v Liechtenstein qualifier is only of *academic* interest'. The adjective *academical* surfaces only in the name of the club *Hamilton Academical*, a club whose small size and modest achievements emphasise, in tandem with the long name, the futile pretensions of anything *academic*. Yet the noun *Academy* is dignified. West Ham United *fancy themselves* in all seriousness as 'the *Academy* of Football'. Many other clubs like to name their youth development schemes in this way, however remote windswept training grounds may appear to be from the secluded groves of academia.

Account: Managers of lower-division clubs drawn against one of the ***big boys*** regularly limit their ambition to seeing their players *give a good account of themselves*. *By all accounts* is the standard phrase to indicate that the person speaking was not actually at the game he is talking about: '*By all accounts*, Tranmere were *full value* for their win last week at the Manor Ground'.

Acquaintance: Players who re-oppose *erstwhile* team-mates are said, often with a hint of irony, to *renew their acquaintance* with them. See also *warm welcome*. For more friendly circumstances, where a player *links up* with a former manager, the two parties tend to *renew their association* or *join up* once more. Although, on an off day, team-mates can play as if they have *only just met*.

Acquisition: Perhaps the most common synonym for *signing*. Clubs always *parade* or **unveil** their *recent acquisitions*, usually at a *hastily convened* press conference. Note though that some adjectives (like *astute* and *record*) more readily qualify *signing* not *acquisition*.

Acrobatic: An adjective often heard in commentary, even for actions which are not particularly *acrobatic*. Reserved especially for *overhead kicks* or *last-ditch clearances*. There can be a pejorative tinge when used of saves: 'Miklosko made that one look *acrobatic*'. See also *one for the cameras*.

Adjudged: For some reason much more common than 'judged' when describing a refereeing decision: 'Grimandi was *adjudged* to have pulled Yorke back'. Takes the adverbs *rightly* or *harshly*.

Admission money: Unit of value for an *outrageous* piece of skill: 'That *drag back* from Zola was worth the *admission money* alone'. Uttered particularly by commentators who have not had to pay the *price of admission*.

Advantage: When a referee allows play to continue after a foul, to the *advantage* of the aggrieved team, fans and commentators alike are so amazed he did not blow his whistle when he could have done so that the *advantage* is qualified as *good* or even *excellent*: 'The Spennymoor official having played an *excellent advantage*, Zico swung in a low cross and Eder made it 2-0'. The referee momentarily seems to become a player here, as once illustrated at Anfield when Mike Reid celebrated after an *advantage* he had *played* resulted in a goal. If the *advantage* does not *accrue* (a phrase more used in rugby) the ref is blamed for not *blowing up* rather than being criticised for a 'bad advantage', which would indeed sound strange.

Advert: Footballers have long since featured in commercials for male essentials – beer and shaving cream – but they can advertise the game itself: a thrilling match may be described as a *good advert for football*. This is more common than the now rather risible 'football was the winner today'. Sometimes, more specifically, a good game advertises the league, country or even continent in which it is being played: 'A storming first half – it's a *great advert* for the Nationwide first division'; 'The way Cameroon reached the quarter-final made it a disappointing *advert* for the game in Africa as a whole'.

Aerial: The idea of *aerial bombardment* or *aerial onslaught* compares teams of the Charles Hughes school of football to the squadrons of 'Bomber' Harris. More commonly, the adjective is used to describe a particular *aerial tussle* or *aerial **battle*** between two players.

Affair: Generally a synonym for *match*, which can range from the jolly *all-ticket affair* (once more worthy of note when you could usually just turn up and pay at the ***gate***), through the *drab* or *lifeless affair*, to the *physical* or ***ill-tempered** affair*.

Afford: The verb invariably employed when somebody has *mythical* or *legendary* status at a club: 'Craig

Madden is *afforded legendary* status at Gigg Lane'. A team can also *afford the **luxury*** of missing penalties or chances if they ultimately win.

Afters: Resumes the idea of *after* the tackle or challenge: 'There was a little bit of *afters* there between Mulryne and Magilton'. *Afters* can come before ***handbags***, perhaps counter-intuitively.

Agony: In its original sense used to describe the last moments before death, *agony* has been cheapened by more frequent general usage and diluted further by football, where it tends (in a strange meeting of the psychological and the physical) to be *piled on* by the opponents. A late sending off or the news of ***results elsewhere*** may even ***compound*** *the agony*. The adverb is almost always used of shots that just miss the target: 'Johanssen's follow-up trickled *agonisingly* wide'.

All about: 'That's what this ***football club*** is *all about*'. Managers, players and sometimes fans will use these summary words when swelling with pride about a spirited fightback, a tenacious rearguard action, a heroic collective effort in clearing the pitch of snow. But when, more commonly, you are shaking your head and commenting on an embarrassing defeat, it is customary to say something like: 'That's Ayr United *for you*' or 'that's Manchester City *all over*'. See also ***way***.

All-action: Used adjectivally by *all-action* prose stylists of ***live wires*** and their *displays* or *performances*: 'Rookie Wayne Routledge was crowned king of the Palace as his *all-action display* grounded *nine-**man*** Bluebirds'.

All of: Emphasises the full distance a ball or player has travelled, as if the commentator has physically paced out the distance: 'Livi striker David Fernandez laid the ball back to Jamie McAllister, who thundered an unstoppable left-footed shot past Gordon Marshall from *all of* 25 yards'; 'Edu ran *all of* thirty yards to get involved there, Martin'. Compare *fully*.

Almighty: Some say football is an 'implicit religion'. Much vocabulary (*faithful*, *fanatic*) would have you believe that this is right. But *almighty* is used almost exclusively in football parlance to describe the very secular occurrence known as the *almighty scramble*.

Altercation: A rather euphemistic way of describing a *bust-up,* a *dust-up*, a *situation* where players square up, as in: 'Bit of an *altercation* off the ball there'. See also *handbags*.

Always: Used, always in hindsight, to suggest an action was predestined: 'His header was *always* going wide'. An *emphatic* finish can be celebrated in similar fashion: 'That was going in *from the moment* the ball left Bobby Charlton's *boot*'.

Ambassador: Certain players have the qualities to merit being described as *great ambassadors* for the *club*, *game*, or *sport*. Pele, Franz Beckenbauer, Bobby Charlton and Bobby Moore are some of the usual suspects when it comes to receiving this epithet (or epitaph). Perhaps Pele's credentials might need to be reviewed in the light of the following: 'He's been such a great *ambassador for the game* that it's sad to see Pele doing adverts for the treatment of erectile dysfunction'.

Ambition: In football, *ambition* means 'money'. It is standard practice for a player to identify a *lack of ambition* as the reason for his leaving a club and equally conventional to praise his new paymasters as a *club with ambition*. No doubt it would sound heart-less to turn your back on a club 'because it's got no money' and a little vulgar to sign for a club because 'they're paying me shedloads', but such sincerity would be refreshing. So often mocked for their ingenuous language, footballers learn their lines impeccably when it comes to the bottom line.

Ambitious: Pejorative when used in the course of a game, to describe overhit passes, abortive one-twos or improbable *long-range* **efforts**. But the adjective is positive when referring to managers, especially when they are young (and Scottish): 'He's a young, *ambitious* manager who wants to win things with this club'. It may sound as though there are other managers who do *not* want to win things, but an *ambitious* manager, and *the direction* the club is *going in*, constitute an integral part of the **set-up** lauded by new signings.

Annals: The conventional phrase is *annals of history*, which can be adapted to fit in with specific club **traditions**: 'This one will *go down in the annals* of *big European nights* at Anfield'. These *annals* are a mercifully sober alternative to the 'halls of fame', imagined or real, that certain clubs dazzled by American spin are beginning to construct.

Anonymous: Describes a player, generally of star quality, who **disappears** and fails to *produce his form* in a game. The usage requires, of course, that the *anonymous* player is named: 'John Salako was absolutely *anonymous* today'. An alternative is *AWOL*, which can also be used of a specific piece of bad marking: 'Biscan went *AWOL* at that corner'.

Another day: In immediate post-match press conferences, even though the manager is being asked to comment on this particular day, he starts talking about another one: '*On another day* we could have had three or four'; '*On another day* we could have got something out of it'. *On their day* is a similar phrase that works to exonerate a team that hasn't played to its potential: '*On their day*, Everton can give anyone a game, but they *rolled over* too easily here at St Mary's'.

Answer: Players like to *answer their critics* by letting their *football do the talking*. A more common usage occurs when teams are struggling for a response to a particular *goal threat*: 'The Chinese really have *no answer* to Ronaldo'. If the Chinese had found the *answer* they would have *nullified* Ronaldo, whereas if they had found a *reply*, it would have been at the other end. Witness the example: 'Li Tie *replied* on the hour'.

Anywhere: A common exhortation on the football pitch when you want one of your players to hit *Row Z* rather than trying anything *too clever*. Occasionally, partisan commentators will also let the phrase slip out if an English team is hanging on in the dying minutes: '*Anywhere* will do now, Tony'. In an **almighty** *scramble*, the words '*could* have *gone anywhere*' are used of the ball once it is safe to assume it will not end up somewhere dangerous.

Aplomb: A goalscorer is said to *finish with aplomb* when it looks as though he knows what he is doing. A finish 'without aplomb' is never remarked upon, but *they all count*.

Aristocrats: Adopted to describe wealthy and famous clubs, without the irony or resentment you might expect of football commentators. 'When Derby travel to Madrid, to meet the *aristocrats* of Spanish football…'.

Armchair fan: Televised football has created the *armchair fan* (he may well be a fan of armchairs, but that's not the main sense), a sedentary species even lower down the scale than the *fair-weather fan*, though neither is quite as annoying as the *nouveau fan*.

Ask: Becoming common in manager-speak when teams take on a difficult *assignment*: 'To come here and get *something* from the game with our injuries and suspensions was a *big ask*'. There is also a helpful phrase for reporting on an *ambitious* pass to a runner: 'That one from Carl Hoddle *asked a lot* of Gary Bull'. A *woeful* pass *asks* an *awful lot*.

Aspirations: In football journalism teams never seem to have title 'dreams' or play-off 'hopes', but always *aspirations*. These *aspirations* are *tested* when the side in question takes on other aspirants, and *dented* if they lose.

Assemble: Managers who are rebuilding their squad, usually through a combination of *wheeling and dealing* and *nurturing young talent*, should be described in terms suggestive of Henry Ford: 'Harry's in the process of *assembling* an excellent side down there on the South Coast'.

Assist: Ugly neologism minted by the fantasy football industry (perhaps via North American sports like ice-hockey and basketball) to denote the *contribution* of a player who sets up a goal. The noun is mandatory, as in 'Alexandersson provided Radzinsky with an *assist*' rather than 'Alexandersson assisted Radzinsky'. Available too in Italy, where it looks a particularly sore thumb: 'Avendo ricevuto un *assist* di Legrottaglie, Di Vaio ha potuto segnare il punto della vittoria'.

Atmosphere: A noun unthreatened by synonyms (never say 'ambience'), but, for variety, it can take a number of different adjectives: *electric*, *red-hot*, *pressure cooker*, *super-charged*, *powder-keg*, *carnival*. In cup finals players go out on the pitch to *sample* or *soak up* the *big-match atmosphere*. Conversely, *a distinct lack of atmosphere* can be remarked upon. *Atmosphere* is usually *generated*, or, more rarely, *stoked up*, by home fans.

Attempt on goal: Alternative to *shot* but often used to emphasise the paucity of shooting chances: 'Baldock Town barely mustered an *attempt on goal* all afternoon'; '*Attempts on goal* were few and far between in this dismal *affair*'.

Audacious: Likely to refer, on the pitch, to **chips** or *lobs*. Off the pitch, it may be the club itself that is seen to be aiming too high: 'Darlington's *audacious* **swoop** for Asprilla raised some eyebrows this morning'.

Automatic: 'Delaney has played so well on the right that he is an *almost automatic* selection'. Note how the commentator here stops just short of telling the manager how to do his job: *automatic* is often qualified in this way. Since the introduction of the play-off system, you can also find the following: 'Cardiff must be serious candidates for *automatic promotion*'.

Awareness: The quality shown by players who know what is *going on around them*: 'Sheringham, showing great *awareness*, put Shearer in for an unforgettable fourth'. *Great* tends to be the accompanying adjective for an individual *piece* of *awareness*; *good* for the quality in general: 'He's got **two feet** and *good awareness*'.

Away goal: Attracts the adjectives *priceless, all-important* and *vital*, even if it is far too early in the tie to know whether it will still have that quality *over two legs*.

Awkwardly: Categorically the adverb to use in reporting how a player falls whenever he sustains an injury in the process: 'McLeod fell *awkwardly* under challenge by Hall and had to be substituted'.

Axe: 'Their fifth defeat in as many games left Ian Ross with the *managerial axe* hanging over him'. The situation is typical enough for the word *managerial* to be almost redundant, although a manager can also decide to *axe* a player from his team.

B

Back four: Neutral technical term for a defensive ensemble. Add *flat* to distinguish further from a *sweeper system*. The required quality of this unit is *solidity* and its most likely deficiency is to be *caught square*. If teams do employ a *spare man* at the back, or you are reflecting nostalgically on the old 2-3-5 align-ment, you tend not to say 'back five' or 'back two'. Although you can talk about the *front two*, midfields are never described as a 'middle four': 'France's *mid-field quartet* ran the game'.

Backheel: Usually *cheeky*, occasionally *adroit, impu-dent* or *clever*; if it does not *come off*, especially when there were better **options**, *silly* or *stupid*.

Backpass: If worthy of mention, almost invariably *suicidal*. There was of course a period where we were all talking about the *new backpass rule*. It is sobering to think that recent *youth products* have played under this rule all their lives.

Backs to the wall: Not a cliché confined to football, but in commentary the phrase always seems to be combined with **stuff**: 'This is real *backs to the wall stuff* now from Ireland'.

Badge: The noun used in football to designate the coat of arms or insignia of a club. The mercenary attitude of some recent players (Di Canio, Alpay, Lampard *et al.*) previously given to ostentatious displays of loyalty has lent a pejorative colour to the term *badge-kisser*.

Bag: In plural noun form, a strange but popular unit of measure for *pace, ability* and even *skill*: 'He's got *bags of ability* if only he could use it more consistently'. Strikers can *bag* a goal, drawing out the analogy of goalscorer as **poacher**.

Ball: Any pass that is better than average tends to turn into a *ball*: *great ball, what a good through-ball, super ball*. On the other hand, you can bemoan *hopeful* balls into the box. While rugby will use the singular – 'the guys were recycling a lot of *ball*' – soccer, perhaps less inhibited by potential double entendre, or because possession is less than nine-tenths of the law in the **round ball** *game*, sticks to the plural: 'Agboola was pumping great *balls* into the **mix** all night'. See also **long ball**.

Balloon: A shot on goal is said to *balloon* over when the striker *gets underneath it* and puts it 'high, wide and not-so-handsome', to quote Kenneth Wolstenholme.

Ballplayer: You'd have thought that any footballer might earn this sobriquet, but it is reserved for the more creative, artistic type. Perhaps more common in the past when *ballplayers* were effete figures threatened by *shoulder-charging*, barnstorming, leg-breaking giants to whom the ball seemed incidental.

Ball-to-hand: What managers say when filing their defence against a penalty *shout* for handball: 'Jimmy Sirrel felt it was a clear case of *ball-to-hand*'.

Ballwatching: Negligent defenders are admonished with this gerund: 'Dennis was caught *ballwatching* there'. Distinct from 'watching the ball' though this is what it also means. One of football's *cardinal sins*.

Banana skin: One of the cherished metaphors elicited by cup-draws: 'So Newcastle must travel to the Bescot. That's a *potential banana skin*, Alan'. It would probably be more accurate to say simply: 'that's *a banana skin*'. Besides, when did you last meet anyone who has slipped on a banana skin?

Bare bones: When a manager moans about his long injury list, usually in anticipation of a defeat, this is the obligatory cliché: 'We *literally* are down to the *bare bones* this time. In all my years in football, I've never known anything like it'. The *spine* may well be missing from the remaining skeleton.

Bargain basement: Any signing who has been *plucked from obscurity* tends to be described in this way: 'Allinson was a real *bargain basement* signing but he has proved worth his weight in gold'.

Battle: Military metaphors are endemic to football and the concept of *battling* is habitually used by defiant managers in the *drop zone*: 'We'll keep *battling* away until it's *mathematically* impossible'. *Battles* are enacted all over the pitch, particularly in midfield, and managers often judge a performance in terms of their outcome: 'Graeme Souness admitted, "We lost all the individual *battles* out there. We were outfought and outplayed"'. Note that you are allowed to describe games where violence has been perpetrated by several players on the pitch as a *Battle*. Hence the recent *Battle of Bramall Lane* (when Sheffield United v WBA was abandoned) or the famous *Battle of Santiago* (when *even* an English referee lost control). But never dignify the violence of *so-called fans* by calling it this.

Battle of Britain: Any game whatsoever pitting an English against a Scottish team earns this description. Welsh clubs are exempted, probably because their top three clubs play in the English league. It is an attempt at saying that British *bragging rights* are at stake. But it is clumsy. The English and the Scottish fought on the same side in the *Battle of Britain*. And there is a ready selection of choice Anglo-Scottish battles to choose from. It would however probably be just too delicate to say 'Scholes' second was turning it into a Culloden' or 'Rangers did a Bannockburn over Leeds'. Characteristic of football parlance, the metaphor exists on condition that its implications remain dormant.

Beautiful game: Phrase used by the sort of people who talk of 'the fair sex'. That is, very few people, though some journalists are given to describing football routinely with these words.

Belie: When you wish to commend non-league or struggling teams for a *plucky* performance against stronger opponents, include the verb *belie* somewhere in the sentence, preferably in conjunction with the adjective *lowly*: 'Wisbech Town *belied* their *lowly status* with a *battling* draw at Conference *giants* Telford'.

Belief: 'At Highbury Leeds didn't go out and play with any sort of *belief*'. What the Leeds players did not believe in here was their *ability*, or at the very least their *ability to win*. As with *tests of **character***, teams are often asked to *show belief* in circumstances where they have every right not to have much.

Big boys: 'Oldham hit back in style to teach Brian Talbot's newly promoted Rushden side a *harsh* early *lesson* about life with the *big boys* in Division Two'. It seems whenever teams go up a division they have to adjust to an initial size disadvantage. The third round of the FA Cup is also always notable for the entrance of the *big boys*. When a beating is being duly administered, the *big boys* turn into *men against boys*.

Big match: Like the *match of the day*, once an innocuous way of describing a *heavyweight **clash*** or ***plum** tie*. But, just like *match of the day*, a phrase removed from the language of football by the television programme that enshrined it.

Blast: As a verb, what managers do to chide and *berate* their players, perhaps if one of them has *blasted* a shot *wildly over*. As a noun, used to register the fact that the referee has stopped play: 'Loud *blast* from referee Winter' means he has blown his whistle rather than his top. The signature of Bill McLaren, but used by football commentators also.

Blatant: A common qualifier, whatever the degree of the offence. Used particularly of *handball*, *timewasting* and *shirtpulling*.

Blend: Always seems to be of *youth and experience*.

Blinder: A *blinder* is played by a pre-eminent player, usually, though not always, an opposition goalkeeper when on defiantly good form: 'We should have finished them off, but Thomas Myhre had a *blinder*'. Used more by footballers themselves than by journalists. Perhaps strangely, also used of referees, despite the fact that one of the most tired terrace witticisms is to direct the **officials** to the nearest opticians. The opposite is *shocker* or **stinker**.

Block: Players are said to *block* shots more than they *block* opponents. But *block off* describes the action of a defender you will see in every game where he **shepherds** a ball to safety while getting in the way of an attacker. Used to record either a legitimate piece of defending – 'Delap *blocked* Scowcroft *off* cleverly there' – or a less savoury version: 'Keegan was *blocked off* very **cynically** by Tardelli'.

Blow wide open: Occasionally used of a *defence-splitting pass*, but more commonly employed to describe a result which revives a team's **aspirations**: 'Newcastle's win has *blown* the title race *wide open*'.

Blue: Fans of teams that wear *blue* tend to rejoice by singing songs not written for happy people: '*Blue* Moon, I saw you standing alone'; 'I never felt more like singing the *blues*'. Is it any wonder that teams in red always seem to have the upper hand?

Blushes: Seem to be referred to in football only when they have been *spared*, usually those of a higher division team given a *scare* in the cup: 'Dave Jones **blasted** the attitude of his Wolves players after Alex Rae's late *leveller spared* their *blushes*'.

Bobbly: Adjective for corrugated pitches, inspired more by the way a football behaves on such surfaces.

Bodies: Men tend to become *bodies* in two particular situations: *in the box* and *behind the ball*. In both cases, it seems, the presence in itself of these bodies could be important (by providing a telling deflection or making a fortuitous block) irrespective of human will or intention. *Shirts* can be used in the same way.

Bony: Less common in the era of undersoil heating but used of a typical mid-season pitch where the frost has barely come out of the ground.

Boo-boys: Those fans that barrack or *get on the back* of their own players. They seem to embarrass commentators who think it rather churlish to disapprove of any player in club *colours*, hence both the specificity and the condescension in the term *boo-boys*, as though good ordinary mature fans will not boo a player. Even when, quite patently, a whole stadium is doing so, the term *boo-boys* works to maintain the impression that it is the action of a *tiny minority* habitually given to this kind of behaviour. Commentators invariably itch to describe the moment of skill or, better still, the goal by the reviled player that will *silence* the *boo-boys*, the first stage in *winning them over*.

Bookable offence: A second *bookable* offence is often abbreviated to *second bookable*, in the same way that a second yellow card is abbreviated to *second yellow*: 'Dugarry went off after a second *bookable*'.

Boost: Place the adjectives *massive* or *much-needed* before this, when describing a player returning from an *injury layoff*, or a victory that has *kick-started* your season.

Boot: To hit the ball without much or indeed any finesse. Players who *boot*, *belt*, *hoof*, or, better still, *leather* it choose *safety first* or the *Row Z* option.

Bore draw: Fairly laboured term for a scoreless draw, driven by the rhyme. Conversely, a blank **scoreline** where both keepers have been kept busy is mentioned in despatches as 'by no means *your typical nil-nil*'.

Bosman: Immortal, invisible, ubiquitous, Jean-Marc Bosman must be the most famous mediocre player in the history of the game (unless you're Scottish and prefer Costa Rica's Cayasso). But Bosman has got a whole eponym to himself, as in *on a Bosman*.

Bow out: The requisite verb to set up a reference to a team departing at a certain stage in the Cup. Another of those terms that makes the FA Challenge Cup seem considerably more polite and olde-worldy than all other competitions.

Box: A three-dimensional object transmuted into a two-dimensional rectangle when referring to the penalty area. Some particular predators, who specialise in **goalscorers' goals**, inhabit the *six-yard box*, which is usually named specifically to distinguish it from the larger one.

Boys: Less common than **lads** but immortalised in Mick Channon's eulogies of *the boy Lineker* (pronounced to rhyme with 'wine acre') and Graham Taylor's tautologies involving *young boys*: 'Shearer, Palmer, Batty – they're all *young boys* and they've done ever so well today'. See also **boo-boys** and **big boys**.

Bragging rights: Increasingly common cliché (which seems confined to football) employed in the build-up to derby games: 'The *blue half* of the city hopes to have *bragging rights* as was the case last year'. Cities are divided neatly in half in these circumstances, even when the *fan-base* is not distributed as evenly.

Brains trust: Used occasionally in live commentary to describe a collection of players standing over a *dead-ball* **situation**: 'Roberto Carlos, Beckham and Zidane are the *brains trust* for this one'. The implication is that they are deciding which *well-worked* move *straight off the* **training ground** they should deploy, whereas they are more likely arguing about who is going to *have a crack*.

Brawl: If *handbags* should escalate into a full-blown fist fight, this is almost invariably described as a *brawl*. The superlative case is a *22-man brawl*, although goalkeepers rarely run *all of* fifty yards to get involved. Perhaps because the game has many metaphors of *battle* and fighting to describe legitimate aggression, a real fist-fight is associated with the bar-room.

Bread and butter: After glamorous midweek exploits in Europe, it's always back to the *bread and butter* of **domestic** competition. Also used of teams returning from cup distractions to the routine of league matches. The image neatly conveys the reassuring rhythm of the league programme. As long as teams remain in a cup tournament, the league is *bread and butter*, but, once eliminated, it is something worth **concentrating** on. See also *meat and drink*.

Break: Used of midfielders, both in attacking contexts – 'Archie Gemmill's *breaking* again from midfield' – and, with the addition of the requisite preposition, to describe good defensive work: 'Scott Gemmill's been *breaking up* many of the home side's moves'.

Brigade: Seen in recent years as a collective noun for particular sub-sets of football supporters. At either end of the scale, you may currently find the *Prawn Sandwich Brigade* (described as such by Roy Keane) and the *Burberry Brigade*. The latter are more likely than the former to join up with the ***travelling army***.

Build-up: Tends to take the adjective *patient*. *Build-up play* is often revered as a continental characteristic in contrast to the English ***long ball*** *game*.

Bulge: Nets do this when they welcome the ball: 'Breitner looked up, let fly, the net *bulged*'. A paratactic way of reporting a goal, if you want to convey the speed with which the events leading up to it occured.

Bullet: 'It was a *bullet-header* from Katschuro'. It is headers which attract this compound form. However, when players are said to *pull the trigger*, the metaphor denotes the action of a footballer about to kick the ball, often presaging a crucial and timely ***intervention*** by a defender.

Busier of the keepers: A phrase used to assess the balance of the play when scores are level or a match has been drawn. Serviceable among careful commentators who wish to imply, but not to say frankly, that one team was much better than the other: 'Vale and City fought out a scrappy ***stalemate***, but Musselwhite was much the *busier of the keepers*'.

Business: Used in pretty meaningless ways, vaguely linked to the idea of being consummately profes-

sional: 'He's one of the best finishers in the *business*';
'We really mean *business* this year'. **PLC** should be
used when you are really talking *business*.

Busy: The adjective *busy* is reserved for midfielders,
usually breathless, talentless, **pint-sized** ones. In midweek results **round-ups**, announcers often talk about
a *busy night of football*, perhaps a quiet warning to
people waiting for the weather forecast that there are
more results than they might expect.

C

Calling card: The euphemism for a heavy challenge
early *doors* to let your opponent know who you are.
The Big-Ronism was *reducer*. Paul Scholes was once
told just before an England v Sweden match by manager Kevin Keegan to *drop a grenade in there*. Scholes
was booked within one minute for a **mistimed** tackle
and later sent off for a *second yellow*.

Cameras: *One for the cameras* is a save or dive that is
unnecessarily **theatrical**. Players or teams are sometimes described as having a good record *in front of the
cameras*, suggesting they are *fancy dans* who only give
one hundred **per cent** when the world is watching.

Cap: If a player manages to score after a good *all-
round* **contribution**, he *caps a fine individual performance*. For the noun, see **full cap**.

Capable: The word adopted by commentators, often
notched up to *well capable*, to warn of a player's skills
at a dead-ball **situation**: 'We all know what John
Sheridan's *capable of from here*'. That the free kick is

within his range of capability may also be indicated by the information that 'it is John Sheridan **territory**'.

Capitalise: In football, seen in the phrase *failed to capitalise on,* whether it be a lead, a period of dominance, the greater possession, the wind at your back or some other advantage. If you do *capitalise*, you rarely say so in these words. Rather, you *make it count* or *translate* your superiority *into goals*.

Capture: Used as a noun more than a verb in the context of transfers: 'Their recent £2.5m *capture* from Leicester did the damage'. Form is always *recaptured* when it has been lost, but never 'captured' when it is found in the first place.

Carbon copy: Despite the advent of the word processor, still the figure for goals or incidents that repeat themselves in a match: 'Three minutes later Leonhardsen scored a *carbon copy* of his first goal'. See also **sixpence, slide rule, woodwork**.

Cardinal sins: In St Augustine, among other Doctors of the Church, the seven deadly sins are: pride, greed, lust, envy, gluttony, anger and sloth. At St Andrews or at St James's, among other grounds, the footballing *cardinal sins* are: passing the ball across your own penalty area, **showboating**, making a substitution just before a set piece against you, **ballwatching**, not playing to the whistle, not lining up the wall and not giving your team-mates a **shout**.

Career-ending: Describes a very bad challenge: 'That could have been a *career-ending* tackle from Dicks'. As soon as the possibility becomes real, commentators are far too polite to say so but come up with some platitude, while the stretcher is coming out, such as: 'You have to hope that isn't as bad as it *first looks*'.

Caretaker: Whether used on its own or in the compound noun *caretaker-manager*, this is standard form for designating a temporary or stand-in boss. In order to avoid confusing him with the man who locks the ground up (and confusing him too), the speaker may take care to say that 'Jimmy Gabriel has been appointed *in a caretaking capacity*'.

Cash-strapped: The favoured adjective for clubs in *financial difficulties*: '*Cash-strapped* Clarets put a dismal run behind them to set up a *money-spinning* tie to ease their financial worries'.

Cats: Whether on account of their natural agility or a taste for stand-offish detachment, goalkeepers and only goalkeepers may be labelled *feline*. But there have been but few if any *cats* as such since Lev Yashin and Peter Bonetti. Perhaps this is because of the modern emphasis on a goalkeeper's ***distribution***.

Caught cold: A phrase imported from boxing naturally applicable to teams who get off to the *worst possible start*: 'The Grecians were *caught cold* from the first set piece of the match'. If a team is *caught on the break* later in the game, you may use another pugilistic metaphor: 'Christian Gross was left in despair after a *classic sucker punch* by City'.

Cauldron: Whether through the advent of genteel all-seater stadia or the invention of the microwave oven, *cauldron* no longer seems to be the metaphor reserved for depicting crowds that are large and hostile. *Pressure cookers* also seem to have gone out of fashion (see ***atmosphere***).

Cause: An attempt at getting three points or at progressing to the next round may take on the proportions of an *epic* quest, a heroic struggle. The noun *cause* comes in handy, particularly when this quest was in vain: 'I can't fault my players – they gave everything to the *cause*'; 'Etcheverria did not help Bolivia's *cause* by getting himself sent off within minutes'. In both statements, the removal of the word would perhaps compromise dignity more than meaning.

Caution: *Caution* is indeed required, because yellow-brandishing refs say something like: 'Any more of that and you'll get a red'. But it is probably a bit old-fashioned now that the yellow card has itself become a form of punishment (rather than just a warning of possible future punishment), leading of itself, in some circumstances, to a subsequent ban. At a pre-season tournament in America, we once heard this come over the tannoy: 'A yellow *caution* card has been *administered* by the referee'.

Celebrations: When a *perfectly good goal* is disallowed by a linesman's unsuspected or late flag, *celebrations*, encompassing both the joy of fans and the increasingly choreographed reactions of the goalscorer, are *cut short* (or sometimes *stifled*). If, within, say, five minutes after a goal, the opposition *hits back* with one of its own, the *celebrations* should be described as *short-lived*.

Centre-forward: Available adjectives include *barnstorming, burly, bustling, rumbustious, swashbuckling*. These qualities are implicit in the more general stereotype of the *old-fashioned*, *physical, British centre-forward*. *Number nine* is still an acceptable if outdated synonym.

Challenge: Sounds rather noble. Indeed, the noun is broadly used as a synonym for *tackle* provided it is a fair one. You rarely see a *dirty* or an **ugly** *challenge* (though they can be *heavy*). Just as an **effort** in football can mean a goal as well as an **attempt on goal**, so a *challenge* is a tackle rather than, as you might think, a prelude to such a tackle.

Champagne: Football gets no kicks from *champagne*: 'Carrick is trying too many *champagne* balls instead of keeping it simple'; 'Berkovic is a *champagne* player and doesn't like it up him'.

Champions League: 'You're having a laugh'. It is properly neither for champions nor a league, but these two English words have carried it round Europe, to the strains of that awful sub-Handelian anthem. It does not generate a vocabulary of its own like the FA Cup, though plenty of commentators and journalists refer to the *Champions League circus*. This is a neat way of saying that it is undeniably spectacular and entertaining, but contrived. The UEFA Cup can now be described as little more than a *distraction* while, worst of all, there will be no more European Cup Winners Cup winners.

Change: *Make a change* is used particularly by pundits recommending a substitution which they consider overdue: 'It really is time Mick McCarthy *made a change*'. Managers are said, with inevitable disregard for campanology, to *ring the changes* when making a multiple substitution or a large number of close-season signings. *No change* is what a forward gets if he has been *well policed* by a man-marker.

Channel: Coaches are forever exhorting their charges to knock it *into* or *down the channels*, although it is not always exactly clear where these *channels* are.

The received wisdom is that it is *in behind the full-backs,* where tireless forwards *run the channels.* But midfielders can also operate **up and down** the *inside left* or *inside right channels.* At any rate, getting it into the *channels* is the same as getting it into *good areas.*

Character: Used in particular when English clubs concede an early goal in Europe. When a summariser says that this will be *a test of character* the implication is that the team tested will get beaten. A reference to *characters in the dressing room* can also emphasise the resilient qualities of certain players, but is more likely to tell apart those players who *enjoy a laugh.* See **quality** for another example of singular and plural having different shades of meaning.

Chasing pack: The standard description of clubs with title **aspirations** who find themselves behind a leading team. Almost a misleading image insofar as it might suggest that these teams are collaborating as they hunt down the leader. But the **results** may prove that they can *do each other a favour.*

Chequebook: 'After brandishing his *chequebook* all season, Malcolm Allison is expected to get results'; 'Sammy Chung will be reaching for the *chequebook* again this summer'. A *chequebook manager* enjoys a reputation for lavish expenditure and is unlikely also to be a **tracksuit manager**. Football parlance would have you believe that the *chequebook* remains the method by which multi-million pound transfers are paid. It will be interesting to see whether it goes the way of **slide rules** and **sixpence** pieces, in their an-achronistic splendour, or whether it will be sup-planted by references to credit facilities and BACS transfers.

Chip: *Chips* would seem to be the same as *lobs*, though the latter are more likely to involve – or *take out* – a goalkeeper. The noun takes a variety of adjectives: *delicate*, *exquisite* or even *delicious*; **ambitious**, **audacious** or *cheeky* if executed from long distance.

Clash: It is always a *top-of-the-table clash*, but a *relegation scrap*, **battle** or, when it gets really **ugly**, *dogfight*. The *clash*, sometimes of *heavyweights* or *Titans*, sounds more heroic, but this doesn't mean it can't turn out *scrappy* in the actual event. Even in the days of the **computer**, it is not always possible to avoid a *clash* of fixtures.

Class: As in other sports, *class* usually *tells in the end*. When their team is winning handsomely, fans may taunt their opposite numbers by singing the question 'What's it like to be *outclassed*?' It gains impact and possibly some sort of social dimension if *outclassed* is directed with a northern short vowel to southern fans or sung with the longer southern vowel to northerners. There is perhaps a reflection of the northern music halls in *class act*, an expression reserved for an individual player rather than a *collective unit*. A popular touch, too, in the predilection of certain football managers for saying 'he's *different class*' when commenting on a **complete package**. It seems that the alliteration offered by *classy* in conjunction with the names of some players, *classy Klas Ingesson* for one, spares them the trouble of having to be it.

Clatter: This verb is mandatory whenever a player has an unexpected encounter with advertising hoardings. Also describes *robust* tackles, especially from behind: 'Huddlestone *clattered* Sutton again there'.

Claw: When a team has *restored **parity*** more by an act of will than by particularly outstanding play, they are described as having *clawed their way back* into the match. The other team, meanwhile, will have been *pegged back*.

Clear-the-air talks: When players are *unsettled* they never simply meet their manager in order 'to clear the air', but have to hold *clear-the-air talks*. The presence of agents may be implied.

Climb: Players may be said to *climb off the bench*, a phrase not really warranted by the height of said bench, but note: 'Little Jamie Forrester *climbed off the bench* to make it five wins in a row for Hull'. When a player is penalised for fouling another as they *compete* for a header, the offender is said to *climb all over him*.

Clinical: The definitive word for the most definitive act in football. A way of distinguishing Thierry Henry as a *finisher* from your average *practitioner*. No doubt Arsene Wenger would conceive of a **trademark** Henry goal not as *clinical* but *chirurgical*.

Clip: Alternative to *shoot*, usually when the ball goes just over the bar: 'Moussa Saib ran to meet the near-post cross but *clipped* it narrowly over the bar'. The ball itself can *clip* or *shave* the **woodwork**, or miss by *a coat of paint*.

Close down: Used regularly of outfield players to indicate what Italians call *il pressing* (not incidentally to be confused with the identical French word for dry-cleaning). The phrase can also refer to the action of an advancing goalkeeper: 'It was a good chance but Myhill *closed down the angle* quickly'. The geometry here is mostly in the commentator's mind, since this is a **regulation** save unless the keeper really **made himself big**.

Club versus country debate: To our knowledge there has never been such a *debate* at any time amongst fans, yet whenever managers begrudge a player *international duty* or there are *late withdrawals* from an England squad, allusions to this interminable yet inaudible *debate* surface.

Coach and horses: What you can proverbially drive through a defence once it has been blown apart by either a *killer ball* or its own *schoolboy* incompetence.

Collectively: Whereas a manager laments the loss of *individual battles* or the proliferation of *individual mistakes*, he is unlikely to *single out* individuals after a win but praise the way his players defended *collectively as a unit*.

Collector's item: When goals come from an *unlikely source* they can be designated in this way (or classified as a *museum piece*): 'The goal from Jeff Kenna, his first in Birmingham *colours*, was a *real collector's item*'. When a player scores in untypical fashion, there is another possibility: 'The *rare headed goal* from Brooking was *one for the scrapbook* in more ways than one'.

Colossus: Reserved for players who perform *head and shoulders* above their team-mates. You would expect the adjective to be used of centre-halves and forwards but in fact the position seems irrelevant: 'Inspired by the midfield *colossus* that is Steven Gerrard, Liverpool brushed aside modest visitors'.

Colourful language: Swearing, generally at the referee: 'Any lip-readers among viewers will make out Gordon Strachan's *colourful language* there'. In the argot of the disciplinary bodies this comes out as *foul and abusive language*.

Colours: Used metonymically for club appearances: 'It's only his third home outing in Standard Liège *colours*'. But the word *colours* has come to denote the replica strip or kit worn by fans. Mildly pejorative, it is often to be seen in the phrase *No Football Colours* on the doors of wine bars and other establishments of high repute. The **hooligan** slogan 'these *colours* never run', thanks to the little pun, is more amusing than menacing.

Come through: First-team **regulars** who have been out injured usually *prove* their fitness by *coming through* a reserve fixture. Teams with *Academies* can also boast of *young talent coming through*. Youngsters, once they have *come through the ranks*, are then ready to *emerge*, a verb possibly applied more on the international *stage*: 'Portugal's *emerging* youngsters make them **many people's idea** of the tournament winners'.

Comfort zone: Some definable point in the modern game where any goal by the opposition would be a **consolation** rather than a **lifeline**: 'Once in the *comfort zone*, Ferguson took off Scholes and Giggs to preserve some energy for Wednesday's vital Champions League **clash** against Stuttgart'.

Comfortable: *Technically* accomplished, therefore usually continental, teams and individual players with style are praised for being *comfortable on the ball* or for having *so much time* on it.

Command: Tends to be used of goalkeepers (as opposed to mere **shotstoppers**) who *come for crosses* and *command their areas*, or centre-halves who are a *commanding* **presence** at the back. Players in any position, if they are rated highly enough, can *command* a certain transfer fee.

Compact: Used of grounds, as a polite way of saying 'small', although perhaps implying a compliment to the fervour of the home fans (*quaint* tends to suggest a ground which is falling down but *full of character*). A defensive-minded coach can praise his team for being *nice and compact* if they have prevented the game from becoming *stretched*.

Competition: A striker's tally for the season is sometimes counted *in all competitions*, to distinguish this figure from the league only. Even including the Inter-Toto and Auto Windscreens Cups there aren't that many competitions though. *Competition for places* is usually a good thing (see also ***selection headache***). Whether a player returning from injury has played in friendlies *behind closed doors* or for the reserves, his re-appearance in the first team is always described as his *first competitive action* since the injury.

Complete package: 'Andy Cole's the *complete package*: pace, power and poise.' Manager-speak formula of praise similar to ***class*** act. Listen to Barry Fry's description of Ruud van Nistelrooy as '*near enough* the most *complete* player', which ignores the complication that completeness does not admit of degrees.

Completely: The kind of overemphatic adverb beloved of commentators in phrases such as *completely **anonymous**, bamboozled, out of position, outplayed, wrong-footed*. The most common of all is *completely unmarked*, usually deployed with a touch of self-righteousness: 'the El Salvador defence have left Kiss *completely unmarked* for the second time in a matter of minutes'. *Comprehensively* may sound more comprehensive if a goalkeeper is beaten *all ends up* or a team *outplayed*.

Complexion: Any key incident seems to *change* the *complexion* of the game instantaneously: 'That miss changed the *whole complexion* of the game'; 'The *complexion* of the game changed **completely** when Smith was sent off'.

Composure: Usually implicit here is a situation *in front of goal*, although the word can be used of defenders, goalkeepers or *firebrands* also. *Composure* is usually *shown* or *kept* in football parlance, whereas *discipline* is what you tend to *lose*.

Compound: As we near the end of a match report, this word always goes with *misery* (unless there are other alliterative possibilities): 'Thistle's *torment* was *compounded* when substitute Derek Fleming, on for Kenny Milne, was shown a red card for a tussle with Pars substitute Noel Hunt'.

Computer: The *computer* responsible for the fixture list may be attributed powers of irony that can be quirky or downright vindictive, as when it pairs a manager with his former club on the first day of the season or *throws up* successive fixtures against Champions League participants. See also **sink in.**

Concentrate on the league: Many years ago a manager must have said this in all seriousness after *crashing out* of the Cup, but today it tends to be recited with heavy irony: 'At least we can "*concentrate on the league*" now'. Teams involved in cup tournaments, as well as the **bread and butter** of the league, are said, a bit prosaically, to be playing on *different fronts*. But this image is nowhere near as good as the German phrase in which such teams are said to be *dancing at three weddings* (although in 2002 Bayer 'Neverkusen' were eventually guests at three funerals).

Conditions: Describes weather, terrain or the effect the former has on the latter: *blustery, awful, perfect conditions for football*. Allusion is sometimes made to *underfoot conditions*, but less so than in racing or rugby.

Consolation: Defines a late goal scored by the losing team. So definitively, in fact, that the word *goal* can be dispensed with: 'Bowles got a *late consolation* for QPR'. The diminishing degrees of consolation in our further examples suggest the word has otherwise become a quasi-technical term: 'Darcheville's strike was little more than a late *consolation*'; 'Kowenicki's late effort brought no *consolation*'. Note that the noun, one of many ossified terms in football, is preferred to the verb 'to console', usage of which would risk restoring the actual meaning to the word.

Contact: When decisions are *hotly **disputed***, the main talking point is often whether *contact* has been *made*: 'Although there appeared to be *minimal contact*, Huckerby stayed down'. Had Huckerby *stayed on his feet* to shoot, he might have *made* a *good contact* or *got* a *good connection*.

Contest: Not used much in football as a synonym for *match* (***affair*** or ***clash*** are preferred) but when a goal puts a game beyond doubt it is very common for a commentator to look at his watch and pronounce that it's *all over as a contest*. The *as a contest* does not add very much (compare ***ruined as a spectacle***) except to convey that he thinks the losing team have stopped trying or might as well stop. There is no equivalent ready-made expression when a club sees its season end prematurely after a Cup ***exit*** and it does not even need to ***concentrate on the league***. But it is possible to say: 'Tottenham's season is now *effectively* over'.

Contribution: Managers are fond of this word either
to encourage strikers who cannot find the net – 'All
Neil Shipperley needs is a goal as his *all-round contribution* is first class' – or to emphasise that there is
much more to their strikers than a ***poacher***'s instinct:
'Alexander deserved the goal for his *overall contribution*'.

Contrive: Most common in the phrase: 'Milosevic
contrived to miss when it would have been ***easier to
score***'. In other contexts, the verb is used when there
seems to be minimal contrivance as in: 'Somehow
George Berry *contrived* to deflect the ball into his own
net'; 'From 2-0 up, Bury *contrived* to throw the game
away'.

Courtesy of: Tired alternative for 'as a result of':
'Preston secured the win *courtesy of* a *brace* of goals
by Fuller'. More ironically, it would seem, in: 'Giggs
increased Man United's advantage *courtesy of* a
poor backpass by Bergsson'. *By virtue of* is a close
cousin.

Covered: Whenever we are told that the keeper *had
it covered*, if a save had been required, he would have
made it. The typical situations, therefore, are after the
ball has *fizzed* narrowly wide or hit the ***woodwork***:
'It's just *shaved* the post but I think Porter had that
one covered'. Never say 'the keeper had covered that
one'.

Credit: Given in a generous or patronising way by
managers in victory or defeat: 'All *credit* to Leicester,
they ***completely*** *outbattled* us today'; 'Give them a lot
of *credit*, they kept on *battling* for 90 minutes'. An
alternative is: 'You've got to *hand* it to them'. Commentators, too, will give due *credit* to a team for their
effort under pressure, if they are in the lead and

refuse to *sit back*, or if they are well behind and refuse
to *lie down and die*.

Cross the park: Or, more precisely, to cross Stanley
Park; in other words to move from Everton to Liverpool or vice versa: 'Since Barmby *crossed the park*,
Everton have lacked an attacking midfielder'. Standard in *Liverpool Echo* prose. You can *cross the river* in
some cities, or the car park in Dundee.

Cross-cum-shot: 'Blackpool were ***breaking*** in waves
and Coid became the next to threaten with a *cross-
cum-shot* which improbably *bobbled* through the six-
yard box and out of play'. Impossible to say in a case
like this if the player knew any better than the
reporter whether the precise intention was a centre
drilled *in* to the box or an ***effort*** on goal.

Crowded: Typically, if anybody is remotely in the
line of the keeper's vision during an ***almighty*** *scramble*, the penalty area is described as *crowded*. The Big-
Ronism was *crowd scene*.

Culture: It is possible for a manager to invite praise
for instilling the right kind of *culture* at a club but it
is more likely he will be making references to the
wrong kind: 'I used to play for a club with a drinking
culture'; 'The *culture* at that time was all wrong with
the *senior pros* acting as if they owned the place'. See
also ***way***.

Cup Final: In football parlance all *must-win* games
now seem to have turned into *cup finals*. Managers
threatened by relegation, haunted by the ***axe***, declare:
'Every game from now till the end of the season is a
cup final'. Condescending fans of big teams, particularly Manchester United supporters, taunt the support of smaller clubs when they meet in a match by

singing: 'One-nil in your *cup final*'. The *Cup Final* remains the reference point for a match that really counts, although, to all intents and purposes, it now matters less to the **PLC** than a Champions League qualifier against Skonto Riga.

Curl: Can be used in commentary and reports, particularly when talking of a wonderful *curler* into the top corner. In this case, preferred to 'bender'.

Cushion: Whereas rugby commentators identify the gap between teams as being 'within a score' or not, football observers prefer to talk of the *cushion* that is, or would be, an additional goal, a goal which would *surely*, *effectively*, put the game beyond reach. Leading teams may enjoy a six-point *cushion* over the **chasing pack**. Headers can also be *cushioned*, particularly if they set up an *inviting* chance.

Custodian: Staple synonym always available for *goalkeeper*. Likely to be used with a degree of wry self-consciousness these days.

Cutting edge: The readily applied cliché for teams who play *pretty triangles* but lack something in the **final** *third*: 'Kidderminster's **quality** *football* lacked a *cutting edge* until the introduction of Williams in the 73rd minute'.

Cynical: Widely used of fouls (rather than of the player committing the foul) when the culprit knows exactly what he is doing. If the term **professional** *foul* risks dignifying such an infraction, the adjective *cynical* makes clear, within the parameters of restrained commentary, that it is unacceptable. The fact that an offence is **blatant** does not stop it from being *cynical* in intent, if not execution.

D

Danger: A shorthand, particularly in radio commentary, for a general attacking threat: 'The *danger* was *cleared* by Unsworth'. At *set pieces* the commentator is naturally keen to identify more specifically where the *danger* is likely to come from, whether it be from the *dead-ball specialist* himself or his intended targets: 'Mikhailovic is especially *dangerous* from these positions'; 'Dean Richards is coming up for this one and he's always *dangerous* from set plays'.

Date: 'Highbury *date* for Millers'. Cup ties which *capture the imagination* are often announced in this headline form by excited local journalists, who also claim that *the whole town* is *buzzing* with excitement. It would be possible, but less probable, to read 'Millmoor *date* for Gunners'.

Deadly: Used of a ***marksman*** whose aim is true within a certain yardage. Sometimes twelve: 'But Gray, usually *deadly* from the spot, hit a post with the penalty'. Sometimes inside six: 'it was a great cross in and we all know Quinn is absolutely *deadly* from that range'. Also reserved specifically for Doug Ellis for his propensity to sack managers. Mr Ellis felt sufficiently flattered to appropriate the epithet for the title of his autobiography.

Deal with: On the pitch goalkeepers or defenders *deal with* difficult balls; off the pitch, clubs *deal with* problems *in the camp*. In the second case the voice is invariably passive: 'It's been *dealt with* internally and I've no more to say on the matter while we're still in La Manga'. Despite there being no more to be said on the matter, it usually becomes ***well-documented***.

Debut: One of the many mysteries of football is the eternal importance attached to the identity of the opposition in your first match: 'Schmeichel, who is married with two children, made his United *debut* against Notts County'. Player profiles rarely fail to include such a seemingly incidental piece of information. But the noun *debut* (preferred to the less glamorous 'first appearance') conspires to make it seem important. Journalists who imagine posh readers and don't work for a Eurosceptic editor have even been known to spell it *début*, complete with accent.

Deck: Synonymous with *pitch*, usually when the ball is being *pumped* in the air too much. 'Thistle should keep it *on the deck* more and *put their foot on* the ball'.

Deep: When a ***back four*** defends *too deep* the line it is holding invites the opposition to come onto them. *Deep* is also used in a variant description of a *late show*: 'Rochdale's equaliser came *deep* into ***stoppage*** time'.

Deflection: The two classic adjectival groups are *wicked* (for any *deflection* of more than a foot) and *slight, faint, the merest, a suspicion of a* for a barely noticeable deviation. *Soi-disant* neutral commentators tend to abhor *deflections* on behalf of the victimised team as *cruel*. Rarely are they welcomed as 'fortuitous' or 'lucky'.

Deny: Strikers seem to be more often *denied* by the ***woodwork*** or players on the line than by goalkeepers: 'Saunders rounded the keeper only to be *denied* by the angle of post and bar'. In such phrases, the *woodwork* is felt to exert a malevolent influence of its own.

Derby: A *derby* match can be expected to prove *dour* in Yorkshire and *pulsating* everywhere else. The adjectives *typical* and *real* make the term *local derby* seem for a moment less tautologous. How local a *derby* has to be to qualify as such is becoming more elastic to judge by recent claims for Watford v Leeds (an *M1 derby*) or Niger v Chad (a *sub-Saharan derby*).

Deserve: When you *go over* to a commentator to hear that the dominant team has scored, the following litotes is applicable: 'It's no less than they *deserve*, Trevor, after that opening *spell*'. You may equally use the phrase *no more than they deserve*, although this is also used in a different moralistic sense when, say, a player is booked for diving. In the last case, compare *rightly so*.

Diminutive: A long word for a short person. It is only ever used of players. Commentators will not speak of a 'diminutive stand' or a 'diminutive dog on the pitch'. Smaller *custodians* can be *diminutive*, but tend rather to be described as *not the tallest* of goal-keepers. See also *pint-sized*.

Disappear: The pejorative verb used of flair players who *go missing* when the going gets tough. Football parlance naturally prefers the pleonastic version, as in: 'After they went one down, Joe Cole *completely disappeared* in the second half'. Compare *anonymous*.

Disappointed: 'He'll be *disappointed with that*' is what commentators say when they mean 'that was rubbish'. If this is not tentative enough, then add 'by *his own very high standards*'.

Disputed: The classic term for a contentious decision, inviting or even insisting on the adverb *hotly*.

Disrespect: Used disrespectfully: 'No *disrespect* to Burnley, but we would expect to beat them over two legs'. If a shock victory is obtained, Burnley will then get *all **credit*** from the opposition manager, still reluctant to believe he has been beaten.

Dissent: Remember that dissent is *shown* rather than expressed. 'Poyet *showed dissent* to the officials' is therefore orthodox, whereas 'Poyet dissented from the officials' view' would be irregular.

Distribution: A *service* offered when throwing or kicking the ball to team-mates. As with ***dissent***, always used as a noun, never as a verb. Thus 'Digweed's *distribution* was poor', not 'Digweed distributed poorly'. It can refer both to a specific throw ('good *distribution* there from Shepherd') and to general throwing or kicking ability ('Bosnich's *distribution* was never his strong point').

Dive: It is held to be self-evidently true that, unduly susceptible to continental habits *creeping in* to the English game, footballers *dive* much more than before to *win* penalties and free kicks. There is now even a FIFA-authorised technical term for it: *simulation*. The word *dive* (which is to be used whenever a player deliberately falls or tumbles, even if it looks nothing like a *dive*) has become contaminated for other purposes. It used to be the standard way of describing the action of a goalkeeper, but, because it reeks of ***theatricality***, a quite honest *dive* of a goalkeeper will now tend to be described in other terms: 'Rustu *flung himself **acrobatically*** to *foil* Roque Junior'.

Dive in: *Diving in* looks no more like actual diving than does much of the diving considered above. The verb is used to describe any ill-judged, rash attempts to win back the ball. 'Don't get me wrong, young Titus is a good defender and he's *learning all the time*, but he's got to stop *diving in*'. Defenders are told to *stay on their feet*, rather than go *diving in*.

Dodgy: The terrace chant is '*dodgy keeper*', and this expression does occasionally find its way into press reporting. You can also complain about *dodgy decisions*, or admit that recent results have been *a bit dodgy*.

Domestic: An adjective you see increasingly thanks to the marketing of the ***Champions League***. *Domestic form* refers to recent results in your national **league**, perhaps surprisingly away as well as home. As in cycling, there is the understanding that *domestic* is unglamorous: 'After a dip in their *domestic form*, Monaco will be looking forward to the visit of the Italian champions'. Mind you, watching Deportivo play Manchester United for the umpteenth time in some **academic** group match makes us hanker for the good old days.

Double save: A situation where a goalkeeper *can only parry* the initial shot but stops the rebound. Often coupled with *instinctive* or *incredible*, even when the second save is fairly straightforward. But do not say 'double shot'. If a striker gets two *stabs*, then it is more usual to talk of *two bites of the cherry*. See also *on the rebound*.

Doubt: Associated in pre-match speculation with injuries that may or may not **rule out** a player: 'Curran remains a major *doubt* ahead of Tuesday's showdown'. Similarly, 'Toshack and Heighway are definitely out, while Neal and Keegan are *doubtful*'. The underlying sense is that the physio looking at Neal and Keegan is *doubtful*.

Dressing room: A prosaic title for this location which hides a host of metonymic possibilities, since it often acts as the barometer of feelings in the camp: 'It was a sombre *dressing room* after Jones's injury, I can tell you'. A manager will sometimes wish that he had a *louder* dressing room or that it contained more **characters**. But too many *characters*, and he might *lose the dressing room*, the prelude to losing his job. Or again, a manager keen to emphasise a player's **contribution** beyond the verifiable attributes (goals, **assists** per season) may try to *appease* sceptical fans with this reasoning: 'Viv may have his best years behind him, but I know he will be a great addition to the *dressing room*'. The *boot room*, a step further into the mysterious recesses of a football club, will always be associated with Shankly's Anfield.

Dribbling: Seemingly less common these days, perhaps because too many clubshops sell bibs sporting the words 'I *dribble* for the Reds' (suitable for ages 0-3), or perhaps simply because *dribbling* is itself less common. Although schoolboy coaching manuals still feature sequential illustrations designed to 'improve your *dribbling* skills', the word seemed to go into semi-retirement on the day Stanley Matthews died. These days *dribbling* footballers *jink* past defenders instead, or they go off on *darting runs*.

Drift: Like **curl** or *float*, a verb describing the measured *delivery* of corners and free kicks: 'Simon Osborn *drifted* a free kick into the area'. Also used to describe the intermittent **disappearance** of flair players: 'The trouble with Leighton James is that he *drifts in and out* of games'.

Drill: Used especially of low shots or low crosses into the box: 'Nicky Forster outpaced the Town defence down the left before *drilling* in a *low cross* for Sidwell'.

Drop down: The reluctant action of many *elder statesmen* in order to *extend their careers* is to *drop down* a league or division.

Drop zone: Never 'drop area'. Somehow imported from wartime Special Overseas Forces operations, perhaps because teams in trouble are in need of reinforcements, but also linked to the idea of the *relegation trapdoor*. Teams in the *drop zone* look up dreamily to the *relative comfort* of *mid-table*. Interestingly, at the other end of the table there are *promotion places and* **play-off berths**, but no demarcated 'zone'.

Drought: Used either of teams that are *struggling in front of goal* or of strikers who cannot *buy a goal*: 'Steve McClaren spoke of his relief as his side finally ended their goal *drought* to book a place in the fourth round'. For extra effect, *droughts* should be measured in minutes: 'That's 3,455 minutes of football since Leaburn scored'. Conversely, on a lively afternoon, it can *rain goals*, but a *drought* is more often to be contrasted with *a glut of goals* or, in recent parlance, a *goalfest*. *Famines* are less common, although you can talk of a striker's *lean spell*, while most fans will have experienced being *success-starved*.

Dugout: The unglamorous quarters of the coaches and subs, sometimes (especially abroad) actually dug out of the ground, but rarely these days anything other than a perspex shelter. Like **dressing room**, used as a metonym for relevant personnel: 'The whole Werder *dugout* were up in arms about that decision'. **Nonsense** always gets more nonsensical if the incident which sparked it took place in front of the dugouts. At Villa Park, not to be confused with chants directed at the chairman. See **Deadly**.

Dumped: Verb used for a shock and/or humiliating *exit* from a cup competition: 'Stoke were *dumped* out of the cup by a thunderbolt from Frank Strandli'. Often combined with *unceremoniously*.

Duty: Noun always enlisted with the adjective *international*, usually to explain an absence from a club fixture and to transmit a sense that even money-grabbing footballers still obey a higher calling. For all the glamour and fame that it bestows on them, those who tread the *international stage* are essentially dutiful creatures, and indeed they *report for duty*.

E

Eager: As an adjective often pertains to the willing *target* man, happy to receive the ball at all opportunities, but more commonly inflated to *ever-eager*. In adverb form, used of *derbies* or games where leading teams have a chance to *renew their rivalry*: 'The return fixture between Watford and Leeds has been *eagerly anticipated* all along the M1'.

Early: Managers often insist on their sides *getting into* the other side *early*, without quite specifying how long this phase of the game will be. The Big-Ronism was *early doors*. Compare **first fifteen minutes**.

Earn: Whereas a single point in the league tends to be *salvaged*, a replay in the cup has to be *earned*.

Easier to score: Used with incredulity, and invariable past conditional and comparative forms: 'it *would have been easier* to score'. But when a player does score, commentators rarely say that it was indeed 'easy' to do so. See also ***grandmother***.

Educated: A left foot can be *educated, cultured* or ***trusty***. Right feet are never favoured in the same way. Are the owners of such left feet more thoughtful (Kevin Sheedy seemed intelligent, Liam Brady learned), or are the feet themselves somehow endowed with these attributes? You sense almost that the privileged limb has an identity of its own in the following spoken example: 'Hinchcliffe's got such a great left foot *on him* – if only he had a ***yard*** more of pace'. No-one seems to worry whether goalkeepers are left- or right-handed, probably because it does not matter, though it could be of more than ***academic*** interest to serious penalty-takers. See also ***left-sided***.

Effort: Perhaps surprisingly, an *effort* can also be a goal: 'Notts County have pulled one back, another *effort* from McSwegan'. But more typically, when a goal fails to materialise, an *effort* will be described as ***long-range*** or ***speculative***.

Elder statesman: Adopted euphemistically of an *old stager*: 'Stuart McCall's something of an *elder statesman* now but he still does a terrific job for us in the ***engine*** *room*'. Players who are in reality *past their best* can also be described as *evergreen* or *durable*.

Elect: Goalkeepers can be said to *elect to punch*, sometimes with the sub-text that democracy is not necessarily a good thing and that they should have tried to catch the ball.

Electric: Employed both of the ***atmosphere*** in a ground and the ***pace*** of players, so frequently that the adjective rarely has much charge.

Eleven: Football cares little for Roman numerals. The Duke of Arundel's XI is bound to be a cricket team. And whereas eights or fifteens or even sevens are common currency in rowing or rugby, *eleven* is used comparatively little in football as a collective number. But the motive is sharper when a team is unchanged: 'Ferguson is expected to name the *same starting eleven* for the second week in succession'; 'Sanchez *keeps faith* with the *same eleven* that finished the game at Dean Court'. A manager wavering in his faith in most of his players can single out one of them: 'I wish I had *eleven Steve Claridges* in my team, I can tell you'.

Elite group: Players join this when they pass a *milestone* for club or country: 'Owen joins an *elite group* of England players who have scored hat-tricks before the age of 21'. Sometimes the *elite group* created can be pretty contrived. It is not as if belonging to such a group confers any actual privileges, like an annual dinner, on the members.

Encounter: When a match is exciting it usually becomes an *encounter*, to be qualified further as *absorbing* and *fascinating* or *gripping* and *thrilling*.

Encroach: Has become the technical term for the specific circumstance in football when a player strays into the penalty area as a penalty is being taken. As such it can be used absolutely with the specification of place understood: 'The ref wants it retaken. Someone must have *encroached*'.

End-to-end stuff: Traditional cliché for a *flowing* game, usually when *gaps start to appear* in defences or both attacks are looking lively. The more fashionable alternative in modern usage is to say that the game has become *stretched*. Summarisers are also fond of saying that there have been *chances at both ends*.

Energy levels: In the good old days it was about how fit you were, but since John Barnes started kicking isotonic sports drinks into waste-bins after ninety minutes of sheer hell, *energy levels* is the pseudo-sports science term.

Energy-sapping: Used of humid **conditions** or heavy pitches and reserved especially for the *turf* of **Wembley**.

Engine: Certain players are endowed with a great *engine*, the sum total of guts, *lungs* and heart. More common in rowing to denote the middle numbers in an eight, the *engine room* can refer also to the midfield in football, particularly when players are getting *stuck in. Boiler room* is an alternative but seen, like steamships, less frequently nowadays.

Enough: When a defender does not effect a brilliant challenge but makes a sufficient nuisance of himself to nullify a *goal-threat*, he is said to have *done enough*.

Epic: Often used in fairly mock-epic contexts: 'The *plucky* Spartans' *epic* resistance was broken on 14 minutes'.

Epitomise: A verb beloved of summarisers cogitating on their man-of-the-match awards: 'That tackle absolutely *epitomises* McMahon's **contribution** today, Peter'. Conversely, a reporter who needs to paint a more negative picture will tend to use the verb *sum up*: 'A *woeful* shot – that just about *sums up* their day'.

Equal to it: Said particularly of goalkeepers, perhaps counter-intuitively: 'It was a great shot but Pears was *equal to it*' (when he was in fact superior to it).

Equally at home: A formula, which recurs in the team profiles found in match programmes, for a player able to play in several positions: 'Gallas is *equally at home* at right-back or at the heart of the defence'. It is sometimes difficult to corroborate the reliability of the claim.

Equipped: 'Early signs suggest newly promoted Leicester are *equipped* to survive at the top level'. This usage, frequent when describing **yo-yo** teams, seems to suggest that Leicester have enough kits and spare footballs to avoid relegation, but the equipment here is of course the playing personnel.

Error: 'The first half was poor fare and was *littered with errors*'. Games which are not for the **purist** may be described as a *catalogue* or, with a nod to Shakespeare (not the midfielder released by Grimsby to Scunthorpe on 7.7.97), a *comedy of errors*. See also **unforced error**.

Erupt: Crowds or the grounds containing those crowds can *erupt*, usually to acclaim a goal of significance – one that *breaks the deadlock* or *seals a win* (though in the former case, a ground more often *comes to life*). However, a bad refereeing decision will also cause a stadium to *erupt*: 'Leeds Road *erupted* after Hackett showed Philliskirk the red card'. Perhaps the metaphor may be more likely than it sounds. *The Sun* once 'measured' with a heavy-duty clapometer the noise of the crowd at Wembley during an England v Poland match, concluding that Les Ferdinand's goal caused a noise 'louder than Krakatoa'.

-esque: The suffix slapped, however awkwardly, onto a surname if an exploit recalls the *trademark* of a hero of yore: 'King's neat little *chip* from 40 yards out was almost Hoddle-*esque*'.

Everywhere: 'Brian Flynn seems to be *everywhere* at the moment'. Used of players who are apparently involved at every turn. Broadsheet writers have been known to use *ubiquitous*, which means their subject will have covered *every blade of grass*. Whereas, if a player is not having such a good game, the ball tends to *follow him around*.

Examination: Contrary to the press coverage of exam results and of grade inflation, when football matches are described as *examinations* (do not abbreviate to 'exam') they are always very hard indeed: 'Wales came through *the sternest of examinations* against Italy and must go into the Serbia game with great heart'.

Example: Managers or players keen to pay tribute to the captain of the team will often state, impressively if a little vaguely, that he *leads by example*. Captain Marvel, Bryan Robson, the *first name on the team sheet* (when he wasn't the first name on the *treatment* list) always *led by example*.

Exhibition: Usually combined with *stuff* to indicate a situation where a team can *afford* to play in second gear and indulge themselves with a few tricks: 'The goal meant United could turn on the *exhibition stuff* after the break'. A rare alternative, which is itself rather *playboy*, is to describe a team as in *cigar mode* or *fat cigar mode*.

Exit: Probably commoner as a noun than as a verb in connection with a *shock* defeat in the cup: 'Coventry's second-round *exit* was *completely* unexpected'.

Expose: Encountered in the passive to indicate that a player or defence have had their *limitations* or **frailties** *exposed*. Equally, players who do not **track** *back* can leave their defensive colleagues *exposed* (whereas good *holding* players *protect* them). In David Coleman hyperbole, defences could be *stripped naked*.

Extra man: When the opposition has a man sent off, the emphasis always falls on the *extra man* of the other team, which acquires a mythical supernumerary player. The advantage can turn out to be a burden: 'West Ham, even with the *extra man*, could not beat the keeper'. Not to be confused with the *spare man*, who is the *libero* when a team plays a *sweeper system* rather than a *flat* **back four**.

F

Facet: 'They outplayed us in *every facet* of the game'. Nobody seems to have elucidated what or exactly how many the *facets* of the game are but this is the phrase wheeled out, to include *each* or *every* such facet, when teams have taken a thorough beating. Alternatives are *every phase* and *every department*.

Factor: To every time there is a season, and to every football match there is a *factor*: *the injury factor*, *the time factor*, *the wind factor*, *the experience factor*, *the psychological factor*, *the unknown factor*, *the Ronaldo factor*. Like **situation** or **stuff**, a word that often pops up in commentary without meaning very much.

Fair play: On these islands we leave it to cads like Jonathan Aitken to take up the shield of British *fair*

play. Only FIFA seems to take the concept of a *Fair
Play Award* seriously. Indeed, in our football, it is
rather embarrassing to win these awards, particularly
if you *flirted with* relegation all the while. So you
sometimes see references such as: 'Arsenal might not
be winning any *Fair Play Awards* this season, but you
have to say they are *durable* on the road'. Compare
sporting.

Fair-weather fan: Now that ***roofs*** cover most
grounds in England, *fair-weather fan* is to be understood figuratively in the main as someone who turns
up only when the going is good for his club. But we
can imagine a time when *fair-weather fans* stayed
away simply because they didn't want to get wet.

Faithful: A popular noun to describe the fans of a
team. Used in conjunction with the team name or,
more commonly, that of the ground. It is broadly synonymous with *fans* but adds the implication that
these fans are *long-suffering*, that faith is indeed
required of them: 'The Edgar Street *faithful* saw
United slip to another home defeat'. You can also
refer to *die-hard fans* or the *hard core*, the latter
phrase also hinting that such fans may be *tasty*.

Fanatic: Noun for fans who really are fanatical: 'A
real Derby *fanatic*, Toner flew in from Kuala Lumpur
especially to see the Rams take on Mansfield in the
Carling Cup'. This is because the truncated word *fan*
has come (quite recently it seems) to mean a person
present in the crowd rather than a supporter given to
fanaticism. Similar deflation has occurred in Italian
where the counterpart, *tifoso* (*tifosi* in the plural), has
become domesticated. Now it just means supporters,
rather than crazy fans who resemble victims of
typhoid – the source of this term.

Fan-base: 'Cardiff have such a great *fan-base*, if only they could string together some results'. Clubs talk, like schools, about their *catchment area* (particularly when unfulfilled potential is being discussed), but it is more usual these days to talk of the *fan-base*, which seems to be something more active than a *catchment area* and more passive than the crowds a club gets, smaller in size than the former, but greater numerically than the latter. Perhaps it's the footballing counterpart to a political party's floating voters, or maybe certain clubs will always have to deal with a *fickle public*.

Favour: Usually plural and in the negative in football parlance; most commonly of teams with nothing to play for who ruin another team's chances: 'Well, my old pal Sam Allardyce *did us no favours today*'. During games, a bad pass does the player attempting to control it – often the goalkeeper – *no favours*: 'that back-pass from Edwards did Dibble *no favours at all* but he **dealt with** it'. Court intrigue pre-dates football but *fall out of favour* is often the phrase to describe the situation of a player who does not *feature* in the manager's *plans* at present.

Feet: 'Glanford Park is *on its feet*. Beagrie, **inevitably**, has scored'. Pre-Taylor Report, a phrase which could be used only at Highfield Road and Pittodrie, but an increasingly popular way of announcing that a goal has gone in at an all-seater stadium. Many reporters will still prefer to tell you that the ground has **erupted**.

Fifty-fifties: An economical way of describing the situations in football where the ball is momentarily available to either side. In practice, these act as the barometer of a team's commitment, its hunger, its desire: '"I'm disappointed with that", said Yorath after the match, "they were winning all the *fifty-fifties*: we didn't want it enough"'.

Final: An adjective used in two ways to complain about an absence of finality. Summarisers can bemoan the lack of a *final ball* (an alternative to **killer ball**) and the lack of **quality** in the *final third*.

Find: 'Sinnott *finds* Les Taylor who *finds* Worrall Sterling'. Football can, in these circumstances, sound like a rather poor game of hide-and-seek. The verb offers itself when you want a quicker alternative to *passes it to*, and is therefore most frequent in radio commentary, where speed is essential. But maybe the usage also suggests some **vision** on the part of the player *finding* his team-mate, while repeated use of the transitive verb, as in the above example, helps to evoke a **flowing move**.

Finish: Takes a variety of adjectives, in descending order of shot velocity: for those that **bulge** the back of the net, *emphatic, blistering or devastating* (these *finishes* also tend to be *rammed home*); for those that are placed, *assured, **clinical**, calm* (these tend to be *slotted home*); for mishit shots, *scruffy, scuffed, shinned*; for **efforts** that miss altogether, *not the best of, awful*. The noun *finisher* tends not to appear on its own as a synonym for *goalscorer*, but in a comparative or descriptive phrase: 'Romario is one of the best *finishers* in the world'.

Finished article: Used by managers to refer to *emerging youngsters* in their squads who are *not quite the finished article*. Once the necessary refinements have been made, they become **complete packages**.

Fire: An alternative to *shoot* but, like *blaze*, usually when the shot is not kept down: '…Clarrie Jordan *firing* just over the top from 30 yards'. *On fire* is also a fashionable synonym for *in form* (used of attackers never defenders).

Fired up: More common as an adjectival phrase – 'Tommy Docherty will have the *boys* all *fired up* for this one' – than as a verb: 'Tommy Docherty will be *firing them up* for this one'. *Up for it* is now perhaps as common: 'England are so *focussed* on their opening game on Tuesday that even Fred Street and Norman Medhurst are *up for it*'.

First action: In the era where substitute goalkeepers come on to face a penalty after the referee has applied a *strict interpretation* of the rules, this is the required phrase: 'Bennett's *first action* was to pick the ball out of the back of the net'. But should the *first action* have been a save, use different terminology: 'Bennett made himself an *instant hero*'.

First fifteen minutes: The usual measure (although sometimes extended to *twenty* or even *twenty-five minutes*) for the *crucial first phase* of a match where the home team seeks to *come out of the traps* and the away side aim to *quieten the crowd* or *take the heat out of the game*: 'The first fifteen minutes* over there at the Olympic Stadium in Munich are going to be all-important'. A statement which proves false more often than not. See also *early*.

First five yards: Distance used to illustrate the prowess of players who can *explode off the blocks* and have *pace to burn* over short distances. For slow older players, particularly Paul McGrath and Teddy Sheringham in recent times, *the first five yards* are *all in the head*.

First name: Inspirational players can be described as the *first name on the team sheet*. When particularly

attentive **man-to-man** marking occurs, you may say
that the defender is getting on *first-name terms* with
his victim.

First-team football: Very frequently combined with
regular, and the stated reason for most transfer moves
by *fringe players*. There is also *nothing* like *first-team
football* to hone a player's fitness, no matter how many
reserve games he has *under his belt*.

First time: As in *first time* shot or cross. Appears most
regularly in retrospect when a player has *squandered*
the opportunity by taking an *extra touch*: 'He should
have shot *first time* instead of trying to *walk* it in'.

First touch: Ranges from *abysmal* to *exquisite*. Skil-
ful players tend to have a *sure* or *assured first touch*.
Another way of putting it is *instant control*. More prosaic talents tend to be *let down* by theirs. In crowd vernacular, particular objects of derision are chided for
having *the first touch of a rapist*. Nor can they *trap a
bag of cement*. For such players, the *second touch* is a
tackle.

Fitness test: Almost invariably **late** (you never hear
of a club booking in a player for a test at 2.30 four
days before a match), and usually to be *undergone* by
the **doubtful** player.

Flag-happy: Classic cliché for a linesman who does
not give the attackers the *benefit of the doubt* in offside
decisions. *Whistle-happy* referees are more often
described as *officious* or *fussy*.

Flattered: What polite footballers keen, very keen in
fact, to move to a bigger club profess to be when one
such comes calling. 'I'm *flattered* by United's *interest*
(*obviously* may be added for further effect) but I

remain on County's *books* at this moment in time'. This *interest*, the inevitable prelude to an *approach*, can take different metaphorical forms, but courtship is the most recognisable one, as in: 'Cissé has already snubbed the *advances* of several European top clubs to move to Anfield'. *Flatter to deceive* is less common a phrase now, but may be used of teams that **huff and puff**, lack a **cutting edge** and are not quite the *sum of their parts*.

Flick-on: While a player can be described as *full of tricks and flicks*, in commentary the reference tends to be *flick-on* rather than just a flick, especially when a centre-forward backheads a long goal kick or someone like Steve Bould *gets a touch* on a near-post corner. The Big-Ronism for the latter case was *eyebrows*.

Floodlight failure: A rare occurrence these days but this remains the set phrase, never 'floodlight breakdown', 'power failure', or 'blackout', always the alliterative *floodlight failure*. Floodlights may however be abbreviated to *lights* in such phrases as 'West Ham are brilliant *under the lights* at Upton Park', not that there are many such phrases. *Big European nights* sometimes seem more exciting, perhaps because they trace their heritage to nights *under the lights* at Wolves in the 1950s. From a fan's perspective, when sighting the *glow of the lights* at an away ground of a certain vintage, you know you are no longer lost.

Flowing move: A **passage** *of play* where a team *strings together* some passes, often in an **exhibition** of *one-touch* football. *Flowing movement* can also be used.

Fly: To *let fly* is to shoot with force, usually from a specified distance: 'Lorimer *let fly* from 25 yards'.

Studs may also *fly* in goalmouth scrambles of the ***almighty*** variety.

Follow: English footballers, unlike English cricketers, do not 'follow on'. But they do *follow through*, when adding a foul to a tackle, or, more bluntly, *leaving their foot in there*. They may also *follow up*, meaning *to score*: 'The Brentford keeper spilled the ball, and there was Nogan to *follow up*'. When the home ***faithful*** travel away they become a *following*: 'A tremendous *following* from Newcastle here in Barcelona …'. But those who say they *follow* a particular club rarely wish to mean that they *follow* the team on its travels. This implies a degree of detachment which distinguishes them from *fans*.

Football: An adjective for a little extra emphasis in a variety of contexts: 'We were taught a real *football* ***lesson*** out there today'; 'he has a first-class *football* brain'. Note also the gradation of meaning when *footballing* is used, suggesting ***quality*** but not necessarily fibre: 'There's no doubting they're a great *footballing* side'. The phrase *played all the football* indicates hyperbolically the superiority of one team over the other, often when this is not measured by the ***scoreline***: 'City *played all the football* today but just couldn't find the back of the net'.

Football club: References to the *football club* are beloved of rabble-rousing managers or chairmen: 'He's Everton *Football Club* through and through'; 'That's what this *football club* is ***all about***'; 'No single player is bigger than this *football club*'. Announcements of great moment require the full title: 'Everyone at *Hull City Football Club* deplores the behaviour of this *tiny minority*.'

Foray: When centre-halves enter the opposition half in open play they tend to be described as *making a foray*, whereas they just *come up* for *set pieces*.

Foreign Legion: 'Next week Chelsea's *Foreign Legion* comes to town'; 'It was the Magpies' *Foreign Legion* that combined for the second goal'. The English language is still coming to terms with the growing prominence of overseas players in the game. This phrase both conveys a sense of glamour and some suspicion that these exotic stars are no more than a bunch of mercenaries. Other such familiar, ready-made phrases have been lifted, inappropriately, into football parlance to meet the new demands of describing foreign contributions. Thus: 'Arsenal's *French connection* set up the first goal'. Or: 'Forest's *Dutch Master* made it 2-0'.

Form: *In the form of* is a staple construction in the reporting of football: 'Barnsley are making a change, *in the form of* Dean Gorre'. Usually clumsy, often redundant, it is to be found in some unsuspected places: 'Plymouth have equalised, *in the form of* a goal by Evans'.

Form book: Streets and gardens all over England must be littered with *form books* during the FA Cup, because we all know that the *form book goes out of the window* in that competition. When a cup-tie does *go to form*, the *form book* is never said to remain on the shelf.

Former: Very widespread usage to avoid renaming a player in the same breath: the *former* Albion stalwart, the *former* Spireites boss, the *former* Anfield favourite. See also *old boy*. If a player does not have a former club to provide commentators with a periphrasis, you may instead pay tribute either to his youth or to his

loyalty: 'and now the Ulster *teenager* looks up...';
'Brooking takes it on his chest and the *long-serving*
Hammer *will* find Coppell...'.

Fortress: Preferred these days to the *cauldron* of
old, *fortress* is to be used in tandem with the proper
noun of the stadium, as though it were part of the
address: 'Strasbourg, still without a point on their
travels, have to visit *Fortress* Mestalla next'. Perhaps
this is because, with *away goals all-important* in
Europe, defensive records are at least as significant as
intimidating *atmospheres*.

Frailties: Tend overwhelmingly to be qualified as
defensive, and are very often *exposed*. Attacks can be
toothless, but never *frail*.

Frame: References to *the frame of the goal* appear
when it is *almost ripped from its moorings* by the
venom of a shot. The *almost* is, in our experience,
essential to the phrase. But there is a figurative use
too, borrowed, it seems, from photography: 'Terry
was not even *in the frame* there but somehow got back
to *make the block*'. Here, the defender had so much
ground to make up, he had *no right* to effect a stop.

Free: When players are *completely* unmarked, they
are often *gifted* a *free header*, although strangely never
a 'free shot'. The phrase is used with admonish-
ment when the header is duly missed: 'Chris Swailes
had a *free header* there and should have done better'.
Free as a noun is an abbreviation for *free transfer*:
'We picked him up in the summer *on a free* from
Carlisle'.

Frustration: When a player on a team destined to
lose commits an obvious foul, it ought not to be
denounced as *cynical* but should be excused as an ex-

pression of *frustration* – whatever the circumstances. The noun is preferred to the participle, 'frustrated', and takes the adjective *sheer* or *pure*. 'Ouch, that was late, Mark – yes, *sheer frustration* from Ling there'.

Full cap: In order to distinguish those who start an international match from mere substitutes, it is usual to specify the former as *full caps*. To anyone unversed in football parlance, the image of a half or *full cap* will seem odd. But in football circles these terms are now emptied of any literal, original meaning. Indeed, even though actual *caps* are still awarded, they can only really be spotted at auctions of football memorabilia or on the head of Paul Gascoigne when he **relaxes** at home. A *full appearance* likewise distinguishes a player who starts from one who comes on as a substitute. But it does not mean, as one might suppose, that the player need complete the match. Some commentators, perhaps scrupulously aware of this, talk of 'Mutu's first *start* for Chelsea' rather than saying 'Mutu will make his first *full appearance* for the Blues'. See also **debut**.

Full force: Not as common as in boxing, but used especially when players in a wall are struck by a free kick: 'Murdo McLeod felt the *full force* of that one'.

Fully: An alternative to **all of**: 'Chevanton struck the free kick perfectly from *fully* 25 yards out'.

Fun: In *Athletics & Football* (1887), Montague Shearman observed that 'most footballers play for *the fun* and *the fun* alone'. The *demands* of the modern game have taken all the *fun* out of football, as well as the definite article away from *fun*. The phrase *fun and games* is always ironic in football as it is elsewhere – 'there was the usual *fun and games* from the Uruguayans before the sending off' – and when strikers *bang them in for fun* or wingers *go past a man for fun*, this is a measure of effortlessness rather than enjoyment.

G

Gamble: Managers can *gamble with* an unusual tactical plan or *on* a player's fitness (sometimes the player himself can choose to *gamble*, perhaps with a *course of injections*, if the game is big enough). The main in-play usage occurs when a midfield player has to decide whether to *bomb on* into the *final third* after a potential **lost cause**, therefore making *defensive duties* more difficult if the move should break down: 'Lee Hendrie really should have *gambled* there and got himself *on the end* of Angel's ***flick-on***'.

Game: Denotes both particular matches – 'Albion were never *in the game*' – and the métier, the profession: 'Robson has been *in the game* long enough to know that these are early days'. Older ex-professionals (particularly dear old veterans who don't realise how much present footballers earn) like to say 'the *game* has given me a great life'. Note also the phrase to denote a team or player who has been given a ***torrid time***: 'Palace left-back Gary Borrowdale certainly knew he'd *been in a game*'.

Gate: Less common these days to describe the attendance at a game (as in *average gate* or *gate receipts*), perhaps now that the size of the *gate* matters less than replica shirt revenues and TV rights, or because the modern turnstiles that clubs try to get fans through look less like *gates*.

Gel: Once a noun spread on the hair of footballers, now a verb which crops up at the beginning of the season as new players *bed in*: 'Once Chelsea's new superstars begin to *gel*, they'll be quite a team'.

Genuine: Failed attempts at gaining possession which result in a foul and are therefore not to be classed as **cynical** should be categorised as *genuine attempts* for the ball.

Get a hand: When goalkeepers *get a hand to it* (*it* being the ball or shot), this phrase must always be followed by the conjunction *but*: 'Digby *got a hand* to it, *but* couldn't stop Durie from adding to his *tally*'.

Get hold: When a shot *travels*, it is customary to say 'he really *got hold* of that one'. Equally, if an **effort** *on goal* is *scuffed*, you can say 'he didn't *get hold* of that at all'. It is understood that getting hold of the ball does not mean *handling* it.

Gift-wrapped: Commentators at work over Christmas often resort to metaphors involving gifts or *gift-wrapped* chances when it comes to describing defensive lapses: 'Nat Lofthouse accepted the *early Christmas gift* from the Blackburn defence with glee, firing unstoppably into the back of the net'. In the same vein, a good goalkeeper who keeps *a clean **sheet*** is likely to be called *Scrooge*: 'Nicky Johns, a veritable *Scrooge* for the Addicks, didn't let anything by him'. But note *Christmas trees* can be seen all the year round in football, as they are a formation not a decoration.

Gilt-edged: Describes a good chance (usually missed) either in front of goal or in a title race: 'Heaney missed a couple of *gilt-edged* chances'; 'It was a *gilt-edged* opportunity to go top'. Although a *gilt-edged* chance might seem less costly a miss than a *golden* one, they are pretty much interchangeable.

Give and go: *Touch and go* is heard in the treatment room, *Wash and Go* seen in the dressing room, *give and go* admired on the pitch. The busy staccato phrase describes a particular action, a sort of **one-two** without the two, while the phrase *pass and move* refers to a team given to such actions: 'Under McGhee, they were a really good *pass and move* team, but now they're just **route one merchants**'. *Kick and rush* was before our time.

Given: Connected with penalty awards, particularly in the phrase *seen those given*, when a commentator or summariser agrees with the referee that it is not a **stone-cold** penalty but thinks there may have been **contact**: 'It was questionable whether Knight did take the man but I've *seen those given*, Martin'.

Gleefully: An adverb like *gleefully* is often called into service when a striker accepts a **gift-wrapped** chance, **slots** *home* or **makes no mistake**: 'Bakayoko pounced on the mistake and *gleefully* slotted home'. The adverb is a little misleading in that the glee tends to come after the goal. Rarely do you see strikers beaming as they hit the ball, like a cyclist raising his arms in triumph before he crosses the line. Similarly goalkeepers are described as *despairing* when they dive for a shot that beats them, even though there are not normally signs of outward despair (at least until the ball has hit the back of the net).

Glorious: Oddly enough, used chiefly of chances or opportunities when they are not taken: 'It was a *glorious* chance to break the deadlock, but Agana *spooned it*'.

Gloss: When a winning team has suffered some set-back, usually an injury, a sending off or a yellow card which earns a suspension, this is the required term: 'Vieira's rush of blood *took the gloss off* Arsenal's victory'. It is usual, furthermore, to add regretfully at the end of the report: 'but tomorrow's headlines will be *all about* Vieira'. For similar but more serious circumstances, when the *gloss* comes off comprehensively, see also **mar**.

Go down: *Going down* is perhaps the most common way of saying 'being relegated'. It is certainly the most common way of singing it (in the direction of the troubled club's *long-suffering* fans). In commentary, 'it *goes down* as a chance' and 'that has to *go down* as a miss' are frequent locutions. The verb is perhaps supposed to confer an official status on the chance or miss in question. A diving player is said to *go down* too easily.

Goal of the season: Brilliant goals are described, particularly during live commentary, in this way: 'What a strike! That has to be a *contender for goal of the season*'. *Contender* is often preceded by *early*, even when the season is far progressed.

Goalhanging: Gerund reserved for the behaviour on those schoolyards where the offside laws have no jurisdiction. Never used in the professional game without irony.

Goalscorer's goal: The sort of goal *goalscorers* score – by inference, an unspectacular one. The tautology may be tautologised yet further by adding the adjective *real*: 'Lineker has **poached** another. This one was a *real goalscorer's goal*'.

Goalscoring opportunity: Since the change in laws, always takes *clear* in *situations* where players *deny* such an *opportunity* illegally, therefore incurring a **straight** red.

Good time to score: Traditionally, on the **stroke of half-time**. Yet, as pundits often duly confirm, it's not as if there is *a bad time to score*. The supplementary remark suggests that a *good time to score* is now one of those phrases which are stored in a mental box labelled 'to be used self-consciously'.

Good work: Can be used to praise an adroit piece of defensive play but more commonly describes penetrative running in the **build-up** to a goal: 'Arveladze *bagged* the second after *good work* by Fernando Ricksen'.

Got down well: What tall keepers have done when making a save. This is spelt out further in such phrases as '*he got down well* for *such a big man*'. *To his left* or *to his right* can be added to provide extra information for radio listeners.

Got good distance: In any situation where a keeper *elects to punch* and the outcome is successful, this tends to be the set phrase. We have never heard a commentator describe a goalkeeper's *kicking* in this way.

Grab: Sounds dramatic, at the very least stealthy, but sometimes used in a fairly neutral narrative way: 'The striker *grabbed* his second goal in stylish fashion just before the break'. But see **smash-and-grab raid**.

Grace: Nice verb employed almost exclusively in the past tense, usually with a hint of nostalgia: 'Redfern Froggatt, who *graced* Hillsborough for so many years,

…'. Players who *grace* a ground have to have played pretty well. They are more likely to be *legends* than *loyal* **servants**, two of the nouns available in football parlance when assessing a past player.

Grandmother: Commentators and summarisers will often tease one another in indicating just how profligate a miss was – 'Even you could have *stuck* that one *away*, Alan' – but there are misses of such magnitude that *grandmother* needs to be wheeled in: 'Gary will be *so* **disappointed** with that miss – I think my *grandmother* could have knocked that in *with her eyes shut*'.

Gravity, low centre of: A player with a low centre of gravity is understood to be **diminutive**. However, the statement is not just a euphemism for 'short', but a tribute to his balance and solidity.

Grey hairs: When managers are not visibly pulling their hair out, you may nevertheless resort to saying: 'That piece of defending will give Ian Branfoot *a few more grey hairs*'.

Grind out: How you achieve a result by **ugly** methods.

Groundshare: A notion alien to the British psyche, stranger than sharing your wife with another man (especially if he supports the same team as you). Hence any proposal for a *groundshare* by a commercially minded chairman will not exactly *appease the fans*. Although you could talk about 'sharing a ground', the compound form in which noun and verb cling together in one word, *groundsharing*, is preferred, perhaps making the idea seem more particular and perverse.

Group of Death: A regular visitor to the language of football, this nice piece of hyperbole appears whenever World Cup draws are made, but can make an intermediate appearance at European Championships or other regional tournaments too. It is so familiar that commentators promptly debate which of the groups drawn might be *the Group of Death* this time round, as though it were a title which has to be assigned to one of them: 'Cameroon, Egypt, the Ivory Coast, Libya, Sudan and Benin – Group Three certainly looks *the Group of Death* in the African Zonal Qualifying'.

Guide: When a team finishes in a respectable position, about fourth in the league, the manager can be said to have *guided* them. Any higher, and he is likely to have *led* the team. However managers do not generally lead a team to promotion but *steer* them.

Gulf: The noun employed invariably for a wide discrepancy in **class**: 'The *gulf* in *class* between the two sides was all too evident **early** *doors*'.

H

Half-time: Provokes alternative visions of the *half-time cup of tea* or the *half-time oranges*. Teams who have *let them themselves down* in the first period usually have *lots to discuss* and do this *over* their chosen refreshment (see **teacups**). If the camera focuses on a manager whose side find themselves behind just before the *break*, he will usually be described as *pondering* his *half-time team-talk*.

Handbags: Describes a contretemps in which *arms are raised* but which is not a full-blown fist-fight. The more *de luxe* versions are *handbags at ten paces* or *handbags at dawn*. But note a variant usage from Chris Coleman which does make *handbags* a synonym for real rough stuff: 'We don't want to see a 15- or 16-man mass **brawl** with *handbags* flying everywhere'.

Handful: Pertains in particular to centre-forwards who are physically imposing or difficult to ***deal with*** *pace-wise*. Sometimes coupled with *prove*: 'Dave Kitson was *proving* a real *handful* for the Orient defence'.

Handle: The way managers or maturing players *handle the pressure* or more particularly *handle the press* is *part and parcel* of the modern game. *Handling* can also be used in a similar context to indicate whether a wayward talent needs strong or sympathetic treatment, although the gerund is more commonly used of goalkeepers whose *handling* tends to be *safe* or *sure* if they are being praised, *suspect* if criticised.

Hang up your boots: 'I'm not quite ready to *hang my boots up* yet. I know I can still do *a job* at *this level*'. Apparently, *hanging up their boots* is the action of footballers when they retire from the game. We suspect that most of them actually throw their boots away or put them in a cupboard if they cannot auction them off, but the image yet thrives, just as most of us still *hang up* when we put the telephone down.

Hard man: Teams or countries only seem to be allowed one such *dirty* player: 'Ivanov is ***many people's*** idea of the *hard man* of Bulgarian football'. *Hard-tackling* also means *dirty*.

Has: 'Ronnie *has seen* Kevin McDonald making a smashing run down the right. *Kev's* hit a terrific cross and *I've* taken it down on my chest and *I've* just had a crack at it really'. When footballers *talk us through* a goal they've scored, the perfect tense is often preferred to a more conventional past historic. Such descriptions gain in immediacy what they might lose in accuracy. Jockeys tend to prefer the historic present when reliving a race, although you hear it very occasionally from footballers too: '*I'm* running towards goal and *I'm* thinking "Keep it down"'.

Haul: A collective noun for *goals* in the context of a game or a season.

Head: If *heads go down*, so too will the team to which the heads belong. *Heads up*, on the football pitch, is not the result of the opening toss but what players say to each other when they have conceded a goal. If you are Graham Taylor, it's also the time for *chin up and chest out*. *Head tennis* denotes a **passage** *of play* when the ball passes back and forth in the air between teams. There seems to be no equivalently neat expression when this happens on the **deck**, although *human pinball* is a seldom-seen candidate.

Hearts: 'Stags' hearts broken by late Lua Lua *leveller'*. *Hearts* are always broken in football by decisive late goals, and not, as you might imagine, by a crushing defeat or by a sickening injury (when you would use **mar**). Usage in Scotland is of course conditioned by the presence there of a team popularly known as *Hearts*.

Helpless: Managers and goalkeepers in particular turn out to be *helpless*. The former *look on helplessly* from *the sidelines* as their team loses. The latter are **exposed** by defensive shortcomings: 'Shilton was *left* *helpless*, as the ball trickled past him'. Here it means both 'powerless' and, to an extent, 'blameless'. The adjective generally exonerates the keeper, but, to make sure, you may add 'the keeper could do *nothing* about that one'.

Heroics: Can be used of a fine individual perform- ance in adversity but more commonly reserved for the achievements of **unfashionable** managers and clubs: 'Dario Gradi has performed absolute *heroics* in keeping Crewe in Division One for so many seasons'. A variant is *minor miracle*.

High-profile: Interchangeable with *big name*. Adject- ive describing certain *larger-than-life* managers, and the kind of transfer deals they transact, which do not necessitate **wheeling and dealing**.

History: Some commentators would have you believe that *history* really began when the **Premiership** was founded: 'Colin Cameron headed the winner and made Wolves *history* with their first *Premiership* goal'. Others go back to the Second World War as the start- ing point, considering the nineteenth-century exploits of teams like Surrey Rifles and Bon Accord, with their big scores and big shorts, to be anomalous and distort- ing. All clubs have their own *history* in the form of **annals**. But should there be *some history between* two clubs or two players, it is a euphemistic way of refer- ring to **previous** *bad blood*, invariably of recent date.

Hit and hope: Perhaps more apposite for snooker players faced with a difficult escape shot or golfers playing from an impossible lie, but also used in foot- ball either of individual strikes (even more **specula- tive** than when one is **shooting on sight**) or styles of play: 'It's all *hit-and-hope* **stuff** from Bournemouth now in these final minutes'.

Hit back: When teams score a quick equaliser, causing *celebrations* to be *short-lived*, they are often said
to have '*hit back* almost immediately'.

Hold your hands up: Very popular cliché for a player
or manager acknowledging his error: 'Des Walker
will be the first to *hold his hands up* and admit it was
a *howler*'. Sometimes the player does indeed hold up
one or two hands, although the former can also be a
gesture to claim offside and the latter a way of suggesting to the officials that no *contact* has occurred.

Holiday on ice: A felicitous Keeganism to describe
an *almighty scramble* where players slip or slide: 'I
don't know what Ravelli was playing at, Brian, but it
was *holiday on ice stuff* out there'.

Home: A magical word in the English language dear
to its speakers. It is cherished no less by football
fans and players, particularly those of Plymouth
Argyle for whom *home* is Home Park. *Home soil* or
home advantage are prized more than on the continent where clubs will, *groundshare* with their bitterest rivals. You will often hear before cup draws:
'We don't care who we play, as long as it is a *home*
tie'.

Homer: A referee whose decisions are perceived to
favour the home side. Seldom heard because this sort
of vocabulary (perhaps adapted from baseball) is neither vituperative enough for most football fans nor
temperate enough for most football reporters.

Honours: *Honours*, to be found proudly listed on the
first page of a club programme, bracket the cups and
trophies, promotions and record victories that the
club likes to recall. Should a match end with *honours
even*, it's a draw, though a draw likely to be less bor-

ing than a ***stalemate***. *International honours* is the
standard heading on your *CV* if you can boast of
appearances for your country.

Hooligan: Originally, when people could still remember those Irish troublemakers, the Hoolickins, the
term *hooligan* had nothing whatsoever to do with
football. Then *football hooliganism* and *football hooligans* came to be. Now the term *hooligan* stands once
again on its own, without need of qualification, but
for the opposite reason that football is so utterly
absorbed by the term. There may be something like
fascination among those who talk about *hooliganism*,
just as a term like 'road rage' may legitimate what
others would call bad manners. But most people
prefer the euphemistic *crowd trouble* when *disgraceful
scenes* actually occur. Notice also that *hooligans*
always are a *tiny minority*, even when there seem to
be hundreds of them throwing seats across Kenil-
worth Road.

Hoops: Clubs more commonly wear stripes than
hoops. An effect of this is that the few teams wearing
hoops (Celtic, Morton, QPR, Reading) will, whether
they like it or not, be called *the Hoops*. But never call
a team wearing stripes 'the Stripes'.

Horse race: There are never more than two or possibly three horses in a race when, metaphorically, they
represent championship or promotion contenders: 'It
is only December, but it already looks like a *two-horse
race*'. Remember also that the race is *a marathon not a
sprint*.

Hospital pass: Such a common cliché for a bad ball
that it sometimes gets abbreviated: 'That was *hospital*
from Scimeca there'.

Hot seat: May be used to place particular emphasis on the pressures of management, but more commonly just a thesaurus version of *job*. Above all found in conjunction with the name of the ground: 'Houllier had been in the Anfield *hot seat* for too long'.

Hotbed: *The* football *hotbed* in England is the North East. You are allowed to call Merseyside and maybe Glasgow too *a hotbed*.

Howler: A glaring, perhaps amusing blunder, usually the province of the *schoolboy* (schoolgirls appear not to be guilty of howlers), as in 'the Equator is a menagerie lion running round the earth', but known also to occur on the football pitch. The discourse of commentary is a sustained attempt at disguising partisan views, but this term barely conceals some derision, maybe even a little *Schadenfreude*, just as others, like *agony*, betray some sympathy or frustration.

Huff and puff: What sides (not, perhaps strangely, individual players) tend to do *in front of goal* if they lack a *cutting edge*.

Hug: *Old-fashioned* wingers are sometimes encouraged to *hug* the touchline in order to afford their teams proper *width*: 'McManaman should be *hugging* the touchline, Barry, and not *cutting inside*'. Another way of putting it is *getting paint on your boots*.

I

Ill-tempered: The traditional adjective, for some reason preferred to 'bad-tempered' and combined with *affair* or *clash*, to describe a game where *handbags* have occurred or are likely to occur.

Impact: Typically used to convey a negative experience, and especially to describe an abortive, unhappy foreign sojourn. 'Milan, where Blissett failed to *make an impact*'. *Impact player*, often with the additional phrase *from off the bench*, is borrowed from rugby as a modern alternative to the alliterative *super-sub*.

Improvise a clearance: Used when the keeper is out of his area and has to head or kick the ball to safety. Such clearances are invariably *improvised* or *unorthodox*, despite being the only legal alternatives available. Acknowledged as *effective* if successful.

In there: Common shorthand in radio commentary to indicate who has come up for a set piece: 'Ferdinand's *in there*, Neville's *in there*, Silvestre's *in there*'. Players and fans probably yell '*Well in!*' as much as any phrase during a match, but you very rarely see it or hear it in the media.

Incident: Exciting *encounters* are invariably described as being *full of incident* (the singular is always preferred to the plural). Usually there is one particular *incident* to which one of the managers feigns momentary inattention: 'I must say I didn't see the *incident* involving *the lad* Richardson'. Such *incidents* become *talking points* back in the studio.

Indicate: This is the obligatory verb, to be used with due solemnity, when the fourth *official* shows how much time is to be added on: 'Jeff Winter has *indicated* there will be an additional three minutes'.

Industry: *Work-rate* may have rather superseded this term but it is still used to describe the efforts of

players, especially in the *engine room*. If a midfield is
full of industry there may be at least a suspicion that
it is lacking in *quality*. The same inference sometimes
comes across when a manager praises his players for
honest endeavour. However, the word *manufacture* is
used narratively without any aspersions: 'Stewart
Petrie and Owen Coyle combined to *manufacture* a
chance for Andy Smith'.

Inevitably: Employed in commentary, perhaps
inevitably, when a *prolific* striker strikes: 'Phillips,
inevitably'; 'Larsson, *inevitably*'; 'Clive Allen, *inevitably*'. Also used, tipping one's hat to Providence,
when a player scores against his former club: 'Tebily,
inevitably, popped up to score against the Blades'. It is
a way of saying 'wouldn't you know it?', suggesting
something more predestined than 'unavoidably'.
There is also such a thing as an *air of inevitability*
about a late goal conceded by a team that has not *put
away* its chances.

Injury: No-one (with the possible exception of Roy
Keane) likes to see a player *injured*. But there are different gradations by which sympathy may be appor-
tioned when injuries occur. If, say, 'Ferguson is
crocked', this hardly compassionate way of putting it
is likely to be that of rival, or at least indifferent supporters. When 'Big Dunc hands in another *sicknote*',
this may be said by exasperated fans of his own
team. Then there is a whole variety of phrases: 'More
injury *woe* for Duncan Ferguson', '*injury-prone*
Duncan Ferguson', '*hapless* Duncan Ferguson, *dogged*
by injuries', 'Duncan Ferguson has been *stricken* with
another injury'; '*Ill-starred* Duncan Ferguson has had
another injury *setback*', in which sympathy mixes
with a bit of impatience. Injuries sometimes *rule* a
player *out*. The convention these days is to itemise
team injuries in brackets after the name: 'Alexander-

sson (hamstring), Ferguson (knee, groin, ankle)...'.
Whole clubs can be *plagued* by injuries as though
they were contagious.

Injury time: As opposed to *normal* or *proper* time.
Since the advent of the fourth official's indicator,
injury, *added* or **stoppage** *time* is often replaced, for
greater specificity also, by references such as 'we are
playing the second of the four additional minutes'.

Injustice: Commentators tend to use this as a reflection on what might have happened – 'it would have
been an *injustice* had City equalised' – but it would be
unexpected as an outright comment on what did happen. *Travesty* may also be used in the same context.

Innocuous: Qualifies **challenges** (rather than **tack-
les**) which look *lightweight* but cause serious injury:
'It looked an *innocuous* challenge but I'm afraid Big
Duncan now has a **problem**'.

Instinct: Whereas some coaches get a reputation for
being *defensive-minded*, others have *attacking instincts*
which have to be tempered. This is one example of
the way attackers, with their **poachers'** *instincts*, are
distinguished from defenders.

Instrumental: Common way of recognising an individual **contribution** in a game or over a period of
time: 'Kevin's been *instrumental* in our success this
season'. The close cousin is *orchestrate*: 'Benarbia was
orchestrating all that was good about City's play'.

Intention: On the pitch, teams can *make their intentions known* from the *outset*, often an attacking version of *setting your* **stall** *out*. Off the pitch, the idea is
often negated to *rebuff* transfer *speculation*: 'We have
no *intention* of selling Emile'.

Interfering: When a player is not *adjudged* to be in an offside position, the debate is often whether he was or was not *interfering with play* (*with play* is often left understood): 'How could Sammy Lee not be *interfering* when he was lying face down in the eyeline of Phil Parkes?' Chairmen are also capable of *interfering* (*with team affairs* is often left understood too).

Intervention: Can serve as an alternative to goal, typically one that breaks the deadlock: 'But then came Channon's *intervention*'. At the other end, *interventions*, especially when *timely*, are made by defenders or, more rarely, goalkeepers. The corresponding verb is chiefly used of those who intervene to stop **handbags** from becoming a **brawl**, be they referees or *peacemakers* (which is what such praiseworthy players are called in these circumstances).

Introduction: Whether for a team or a player usually a chastening experience. The favourite accompanying adjective is *harsh*, as witnessed by: 'It was a *harsh introduction* to the Premiership'. Can be used more neutrally of a substitution: 'After the *introduction* of Wilcox, Leeds had a bit more **width**'.

Invitation: A usage which chides a defence for being so **schoolboy** as to have **gift-wrapped** a chance for a *natural goalscorer*, and simultaneously compliments the striker for his **poacher's instincts**: 'Godden could only parry the shot and Greenhoff needed no second *invitation*'.

Ironically: Study the following three phrases:
  'Ironically, after beating Preston in the previous round, Mick Harford's men now face another round trip to Lancashire';
  'Ref Kim Milton Nielsen is handing Beckham the **matchball**. *Ironically*, Becks was sent off by him last

time they met';

'Dickov, released by Man City last year, *ironically* grabbed the first goal for Leicester against them'.

In none of these phrases is irony, invoked in football at the hint of the slightest coincidence or the smallest twist of fate, really present. Let's examine again the above phrases and imagine circumstances in which they could be called *ironic*. Maybe they could conceivably be thus counted if:

Harford had, as a psychological ploy, said to his men before playing Preston: 'I'm telling you, if you dare lose this game, I'm going to discipline you by putting you back on the coach next week to make the long trip to Lancashire all over again';

Kim Milton Nielsen had on the previous occasion sent Beckham off for picking the ball up and holding it in his hands during the match;

The manager who released Dickov had explained in so doing that he didn't score enough goals. A player-manager, he himself was the beaten goalkeeper. And his wife was born in Leicester. And she was going out with Dickov.

See also **literally**.

-ite: The suffix *-ite*, in common with usage in political language, indicates allegiance rather than resemblance (see **-esque**). For some reason it seems to be more common in the north: *Kopite, Spireite, Wednesdayite*.

J

Jet-heeled: Seen occasionally in programme notes as a synonym for *quick*. Perhaps only in our imagination, but used particularly of players called Jermaine.

Jigsaw: Once a manager has **assembled** his squad, he is often left searching for the *final* or *missing piece in the jigsaw*. You might think that the final piece of a jigsaw would be the easiest to place since there is only one space left for it. But not in football.

Job: There are a number of situations in which a *job* gets done in football. For example, when a player is asked to play out of position and is concerned not to let the team down: 'Keane prefers to play in midfield but can *do a job* for United in defence'. Or again, when a player succeeds in *marking* a key opponent *out of the game*: 'Horne *did a job on* Molby today and that was a contributing factor in our win'. We have also heard Andy Townsend say 'did a *job of work*' in this context. Third, whenever a shot *cannons off* it, a wall is said to have *done its job*. But the wall is *not* acknowledged to have 'done its job' when it induces the player taking the free kick to strike the ball wide or over. From which we deduce that the basic job description for a wall is to be hit by the ball. Meanwhile, *job done* is a phrase which greets any required achievement efficiently achieved, like a penalty *despatched* or a **professional** second leg performance to *seal* an aggregate victory.

Journey home: This is always lengthened disproportionately if the result has gone against you: 'It will be a *long journey home* to Bristol tonight for Danny Wilson *and his **men***'. Whereas, if Danny's *men* had pulled off a spectacular victory *on the road*, the following, highly unlikely, scenario might be envisaged: 'The *red half* of Bristol will be *dancing in the streets* tonight'.

Journeyman: Although great players will make more and longer journeys than run-of-the-mill *pros*, the *journeyman* is one of the latter, moving forlornly between clubs in the lower divisions. The term de-notes a player who has had 'more clubs than Jack Nicklaus', an old quip which is yet to be updated with reference to more contemporary golfers. Those who think this too pejorative may talk instead of, for example, '*well-travelled* Imre Varadi'. For football clubs who are ***groundsharing***, while their stadium is renovated, use *nomadic*.

K

Keep goal: The verb has a rather archaic flavour these days, but may yet be used without self-con-sciousness when you are talking about a goalkeeper of a bygone era: 'Frank Swift *kept goal* for Man City in those heady days'. Modern goalkeepers can how-ever *keep* their team *in it* (a usage provoked also by late goals in the cup). Some fans will prefer to use an inexplicable plural: 'Arphexad's *in nets* or *in goals*'.

Keystone Cops: A ready allusion when a defence is at ***sixes and sevens***: 'That was *Keystone Cops stuff* from Vale there'. *Comedy* can also be used adjectivally in this way: '*Comedy* defending from Craddock and Thome'. But note that when the blame lies squarely and obviously with one player, above all if a goal-keeping *clanger* should occur, and it seems cruel to laugh, comedy tends to give way in conventional commentaries to embarrassment or even sympathy: 'You have to *feel for* the ***lad*** there, Des'.

Kick: The basic action in the game, but too basic to be a significant word in reporting on it. Passing, crossing and shooting are simply more purposeful, so that the word *kick* is required only in compounds like *overhead kick* and *bicycle kick*, having become virtually redundant with *penalty* and *corner*. Only the goal-keeper's use of his feet can systematically be referred to as *kicking*, while attempts to *kick* your opponents *off the **park*** have nothing to do with the ball. Mean-while *Kicker* might appear to be a good English word, except that it provides the title of the main German paper devoted to football, as well as featuring in some of that nation's clubnames (*Kickers Offenbach* is the sprightliest example). There is nothing comparable in English, unless you count Mark Smith's polemic against the football authorities trampling on flair in his *Kicker Conspiracy* – but then Mark Smith is used to playing in Germany.

Kick-off: Tends to be used more before than during or after a game. You would always say: 'Just ten min-utes to *kick-off…*', but ten minutes *into the game* it would be unusual to say 'Ten minutes after *kick-off…*'. *Kick off* is also appropriated to describe the out-break of football-related violence, often with a similar sense of anticipation: 'it looks like it could *kick off* over there any minute…'.

Kick-start: A phrase used by managers when they hope a good performance will *turn around their for-tunes:* 'I really hope this win will *kick-start* our sea-son'. More applicable than **restart**, which serves instead to indicate the resumption after half-time, and more probable than *jump-start*, although this is potentially the more appropriate image for teams whose form is *spluttering*.

Kill off: What goalscorers do to cup-ties: 'It was left to McFadden to *kill off* the tie with his second of the afternoon'. Rarer – although possible – to see such an unsentimental phrase used directly of teams: 'The third goal has finally *killed* Scunthorpe *off*'.

Killer ball: Tends to be employed in a critical way to highlight what a team lacks: 'They've played *pretty* enough stuff *in front of them* but there's no *killer ball*'. For concerns of the same order, you can refer to ***final ball*** and *end product*.

Knock the ball about: A phrase with connotations of knockabout for teams happy to *knock the ball about*, or simply *knock it about*, if they are winning easily and able to indulge in ***exhibition stuff***.

L

Lackadaisical: An emphatic euphemism for 'lazy' or 'lacking concentration'. Reserved for individual defenders or the ***back four*** as a unit. In football, the variant form *lacksadaisical* also seems to be allowed, perhaps by contamination with *lax*.

Lacklustre: Can be said of any individual or team *display*, but particularly of flat, lifeless home performances.

Lads: 'We've got a *great set of lads* here at Millmoor and you can begin to see that in our play'. Not quite such a common term as in the 1980s (it is hard to think of Arsene Wenger referring to *the lads* rather than *my players*). In the singular, *lad* tends to be used for somebody who has been unfortunate or who has shown his fighting spirit: 'You have to feel sorry for the *lad*'; '*All **credit** to the lad* for coming back from that injury'.

Land: 'We've *landed* Lazio'. What star-struck smaller teams say when they are *paired* with one of the ***big boys*** in a tournament.

Last man: Since the change in the laws, the short-hand for a defender who is the last line of defence and could therefore risk dismissal if he illegally *denies* the opposition a *clear goalscoring opportunity*. Used less insistently of the final defender when marginal offside decisions are being analysed.

Last-gasp: Often said of goals (equalisers or winners rather than *consolations*). In the case of a desperate clearance, the more likely expression is *last-ditch*.

Latch onto: A classic expression for a forward either making a good connection or running on to a pass. When they *meet* crosses they tend to do so with their heads.

Late run: The adjective *late* here designates a *well-timed run* (often those of attacking midfielders) spotted too *late* by defenders, so that it works almost like a transferred epithet: 'Scholes' *late run* and *emphatic finish* wrapped up the points for *United*'. See also *show* and *fitness test*.

League: Ten years ago when Juventus, Real Madrid or Ajax won the *league* they won the *league*. Now, thanks to Channels 4 and 5 (and Ryanair), people talk only of *Serie A*, *La Liga*, *Eredivisie* and so on. Similarly, Francis and Souness may reminisce about missing out on winning the title with Sampdoria and dream of managing them to another *scudetto*. Only Alex Ferguson seems to stick to the old style, although he pronounces the word 'weague'.

Left to right: It is a topos of radio commentary that you will start a half by saying that 'Oldham Athletic are playing from *left to right* as we look'. Yet unless you give the location of the commentary box, the information is not necessarily useful.

Left-sided: A phrase used much more commonly than *right-sided*, because of the premium on *left-sided* players (and in recent years because of a perceived deficiency on England's *left side*). Perhaps because of political correctness, there seem to be fewer references to *left-footers* than *left-sided players* nowadays. See **educated** and **trusty**.

Legislate: 'You just can't *legislate* for a ricochet like that'; 'There's no *legislating* against such an **outrageous** piece of skill'. But you can, it seems, legislate for how managers console themselves publicly in such circumstances.

Legs: There are 46 of them on the pitch when the game gets under way, but the occasions are comparatively few for reporting on their activity. When a defender tackles an opponent unfairly from behind, he *takes his legs away*. Or if a winger *has the legs* on his full back, he is just plain quicker. But while footballers can be routinely described as having *good feet*, we have not come across a reference to 'fast legs'. Instead, the most predictable context in which *legs* are likely to appear is when there is a late substitution: 'It may be time for Graham to think about *fresh legs* at this stage in the game'.

Lesser nations: The *minnows* among international teams, once a constituency as recognisable and as pitiable as the minor counties in cricket. Games against them in a qualifying group provided an opportunity to *improve your goal difference*. But now managers or pundits wary of an upset often use the less condescending *so-called lesser nations*. It has also become conventional for such managers to observe, with some nostalgia, that *there are no easy games now*.

Lesson: Always a *football* or *footballing lesson, handed out* by the opposition. See also *examination*.

Level: Especially in the phrase *at this level* and typically for admonitory effect: '*At this level* you'd expect to hit the target every time from that distance'. *Leveller*, meanwhile, can be found as a synonym for *equaliser*, as well as describing what the *playing surface* is likely to become on a *Wednesday night in Rochdale*.

Lifeline: As opposed to a *consolation*, which as a general rule can arrive only when you are three goals down, teams are thrown a *lifeline* at two-down when they score with a few minutes left. This invariably *makes things interesting*: 'Kevin Horlock made it 2-1 to throw City a *lifeline*'.

Likes of: Addition or alternative to *your*: '*The likes of* the Zidanes, the Figos, the Beckhams', especially when you are emphasising that there are very few players like these.

Limp off: Shorthand for a player withdrawing through *injury*, even if the *knock* is not actually causing him to limp. Players still actually on the pitch are very rarely described as *limping*. Rather, they are said to be *not moving freely*, having a *problem* or *carrying a knock*. They only start *limping* as they actually *come off* the field of play.

Line-up: Useful alternative to *team*, particularly in pre-match discussion, when you want to pay more than usual attention to its component parts or to the formation its members might take up. Then, as the live commentary begins, you can switch over to the verb: 'Ipswich *line up* then with Sivell in goal…'.

Link: In the summer months of years ending in odd numbers (no World Cups or European Championships, in other words) transfer *speculation* is all the more rife. 'Rivaldo has been *linked* with Tottenham' is the standard formulation. Usually this means there is no *link* other than that rumoured by the paper where you see this written. Easier to corroborate is *link play*, often *good **old-fashioned** link play*, responsible for connecting defence with attack.

Literally: Like **ironically** and *massively*, massively overused in football. Whether they say '*literally* the last kick of the game' or 'he *literally* cut him in half', there is no guarantee that they mean it, although the first of these examples has to be truer than the second.

Live wire: Often applied to midfielders with an eye for goal, who turn up **everywhere**.

Loan: A few rules apply here: players are not described as *loaned* to another team but are *sent* or *farmed* out *on loan* (the latter phrase is probably better suited to cases involving players *out of **favour***); as a noun, again it is never simply a *loan* but a *loan **spell*** or *loan **period***.

Local hero: Commentators too need to prove themselves *at international **level*** these days and there are formulae which attest to their serious homework or proper acclimatisation: 'Some of the home fans I talked to in the restaurant last night rate their striking pair highly'. While commentating on a match abroad, you do not want to be caught out if the local cameraman dwells for an eternity on some venerable figure in an overcoat who looks like he could never have been a footballer. This personage could turn out to be a *legend*, if not quite an **ambassador**. He can be called a *local hero*, but usually in a qualified way: 'Krankl's still something of a *local hero by all accounts*'. Then you may add a statement like: 'They still talk about that winning strike of his against Luxembourg *in these parts*'.

Long ball: *Long-ball game* is canonical, so much so that phrases like ***Route One*** now seem to be preferred. *Long balls* themselves can be *pumped* or *rained into* opposition ***boxes*** when they threaten to be effective, whereas ineffectual teams *resort to* or *fall back on* them.

Long-range: Frequently combined with ***effort***; much preferred to *a shot from distance*.

Long time: 'The first goal was a *long time* coming'. A *long time* is also the unit of measure for a football player's retirement: 'I try to savour every single moment because you are a *long time* retired in this game'.

Look for it: Typically in the imperfect tense: 'Owen *was looking for it*' – *it* being the foul that would earn a penalty or a free kick. This verb covers the contentious, ambiguous moment when a player who has *gone to ground* has neither obviously taken a ***dive*** nor unequivocally been fouled. It suggests, if this were possible, cheating within the rules of the game. When a player is said to *win a penalty*, similar suspicions are allowed to flicker.

Look in the mirror: If defences have been doing a lot of looking at one another of an evening, their angry managers generally exhort them to *look in the mirror*, or to *have a good look at themselves*.

Look out of place: Almost always negated to pay a compliment: 'Gabbidon has really *not looked out of* *place* at all in this *exalted company* in the first half'. If you want to extend this to praising a whole team which is *punching above its weight* against **quality** opposition, then it is common to hypothesise: 'You wouldn't know which was the lower division team in this match if you had just turned up from outer space'. It is of course common knowledge in outer space that lower divisions exist.

Lose: Not recommended in football unless you are *losing your marker*. *Slip* or *shake* are the alternatives.

Lost causes: 'We were **breaking** with purpose and *chasing lost causes*'. Some players have been praised for their enthusiasm in *chasing paper bags*, which are more material than *shadows*, but that's a futile pursuit too. You would think *chasing lost causes* would be plain daft but in football the inference is that persistence is always worthwhile. Compare **work-rate**.

Lottery of penalties: Commentators favour this combination of nouns particularly as extra time advances. However keenly anticipated, the penalty shootout tends to be preceded by the epithet *dreaded*. The same commentators who call penalties a *lottery* (one way of excusing England's successive failures from the spot) nevertheless invariably designate as the *hero* either the goalkeeper who makes the decisive save or the player who happens to be the one who took the final winning penalty.

Lurk: Strikers with a **poacher**'s **instinct** can sometimes be found *lurking at the far post*, sometimes even *with intent*. The near post is considered far too conspicuous a place to *lurk in*, even if you are amidst a *crowd* of players.

Luxury: There are two principal footballing luxuries. If a team wins despite missing a penalty, this becomes a *luxury* they could ***afford***; managers with a ***selection headache*** can ***afford*** the *luxury* of leaving a star player on the bench. *Luxury* (or ***champagne***) *players* are not a good thing though. See ***Wednesday night in Rochdale***.

M

Made himself big: The most common phrase to describe a goalkeeper's actions when he confronts an opposing player bearing down on him in a ***one-on-one***. Only used in the past tense after a save.

Magic: A word that has lately lost some of its *magic*, but even the most seasoned commentator can still anticipate *a moment of magic* which will *break the deadlock*. At one time schoolyard graffiti might announce that 'West Ham are *magic*' – and perhaps there was even a time when it was true. Now used more of players than of teams to describe feats that would be ***outrageous*** if performed by lesser mortals: 'Zola, the little *magician*, turned the game with a moment of *sublime* skill'. *Sorcerer* is deployable ('that Zola was a Sardinian *sorcerer*') but *wizard*, now anachronistic anyway (as in '*wizard* of the *dribble*'), has been commandeered for the foreseeable future by quidditch commentators.

Make no mistake: Synonymous with scoring, when a routine chance presents itself to a *proven* striker: 'Shearer *made no mistake* from there'. Otherwise used by managers and pundits to buy themselves time to think of something to say: '*Make no mistake*, we'll be absolutely focussed for Saturday'.

Make the most of it: Reserved for players, often continentals, who *go down as if they have been shot* or even *poleaxed*. Interchangeable with *make a meal of it*. Such exponents particularly *deserve an Oscar* if they make a *remarkable recovery* as soon as the stretcher appears. See also, for less **blatant** conduct of this sort, **look for it**.

Make the shirt your own: To become an **automatic** *selection* in that position: 'Sansom has *made* the number three shirt *his own*'. Now that players can afford their own shirts and that these bear names as well as numbers, this expression is less common in club football, but it is still available for *international duty*.

Makeshift: The standard adjective for a player deployed in an unfamiliar position: 'Dublin, the *makeshift* centreback'. Preferred to the adjective *acting*, although you can be an *acting manager* if you have not yet been appointed **caretaker**. Also used of strike-forces or defensive units when a manager's resources are stretched. Compare **recognised**.

Man: Always used in preference to other available nouns (like 'player' or 'footballer') after a sending-off which changes the *whole* **complexion** of a game: '*Down* to ten *men*, United quickly lost a second goal'; 'Nine-*man* Kidderminster held on for the remaining minutes'; 'With Trinidad and Tobago *reduced* to eight *men*, the game descended into farce'; '*Seven-man* Blades were clearly **looking for** an abandonment'.

Manager: Takes a variety of adjectives: *wily, volatile, shrewd, canny, Scottish*. Compound nouns of the type **chequebook-manager, tracksuit-manager** are more contemporary in feel. Vernacular synonyms are *the gaffer, the guvnor, the boss*. *Management* tends not to be used unless it is qualified by an adjective, as in *man management*, or *top-level management*. Some players are *every manager's dream*, while *all managers will tell you* certain truisms about the game, including the fact that any *vote of confidence* in them from the chairman is *dreaded*.

Man-to-man: In modern parlance the locution is regarded as complete without the addition of *marking*: 'Koeman's now switched to *man-to-man* on Völler'; 'After the substitution Tottenham have reverted to *man-to-man* at the back'.

Many people's idea: How *pundits* indicate the majority (and/or their own) view: 'Sunderland struggled against a Forest side who are *many people's idea* of favourites for promotion'.

Mar: The verb favoured by commentators when embarrassed by the need to add to the business of reporting a match the account of a tragedy or serious misfortune – perhaps an earthquake has destroyed the South Stand or a star player has pulled a hamstring or crowd trouble has broken out (or all of the above have somehow caused one another). This verb *puts things into perspective*: 'United's win was *marred* by Pingel's broken leg'. A victory or match may likewise be *soured* in such cases. See also *gloss*.

Marching orders: Given to players who get a red card. A somewhat circumlocutory way of reporting a sending-off, though not as sublimely euphemistic as the *early bath*.

Mark: Used narratively for timings in a game, with a margin of choice as to the preposition: '*On* the half-hour *mark*'; '*Around* the 70-minute *mark*'.

Marksman: Alternative, perhaps not as popular as it used to be, for striker. Goalscorers, particularly if they are in a *rich vein of form* or *among the goals* (a little phrase which neatly suggests the prowess of a striker accustomed to finding the net) can be said to be *on the mark again,* in an expression which combines the idea of a sharpshooter with being up to the mark.

Matchball: What a ball becomes when it is sponsored, taken home by a *hat-trick hero,* or offered at auction.

Mathematically: An adverbial favourite which recurs towards the end of every season. Popular in *situations* (which generally do not involve much mathematics) to denote a remote theoretical possibility: 'This is a giant step for Vale, Gary, but they're not *mathematically* safe yet'; 'After their defeat at the Reebok, Leeds are down, barring the *mother of mathematical miracles*'.

Maximum points: Three points or, more deliberately, *all three points.* 'Slaven's strike gave Boro *maximum points*'. The usage seems more justifiable in reporting pursuits like county cricket or ice-dancing, but is known to occur in football.

Mazy: Reserved exclusively for *runs* or *dribbles* by *tricky* customers: 'After a *mazy* run Huckerby **blasted** over the bar'.

Measured: Adjective applied especially to passes. Sometimes the tape measure, or **slide rule**, comes out and the pass is described as *inch-perfect.* Whereas crosses tend to be *pinpoint.* Shots from *point-blank* range are normally remarked upon when the goalkeeper makes a *reflex save.*

Meat and drink: In football circles this everyday cliché tends to be reserved for situations where attacking teams *play to the strengths* of the defenders: 'These long balls they keep *pumping in* are just *meat and drink* to Adams and Bould'. See also ***bread and butter***.

Medical: Transfers always seem to be announced *subject to a medical*, a useful get-out clause for the acquiring team, and indeed for journalists who launch speculative exclusives. The other tabloid tactic consists of using the preposition *to* when announcing 'Zidane *to* sign for Spurs'. An indefinite future is masked by that useful little word.

Men: Note the journalistic fondness for saying 'Danny Wilson *and his men*' rather than Bristol City, more to vary the discourse than to evoke team spirit.

Mentally: Adverb used with *prepared*, *ready* or *up for it*, sometimes *right* or *strong*, and even *gone* or *lost it*.

Merchant: A journalistic standby, as in these two phrases noted in the same edition of one paper: 'Owen is no longer simply a *head-down merchant*'; 'Arsenal have got to steel themselves against *the wind-up merchants*'.

Midfield: Historically there was no such thing as a *midfield* as long as a team possessed a self-respecting half-back line. Nowadays the *midfield* area is *packed* with its own *ever-willing* terminology. Individual *midfielders* can be variously described as *dervishes* or *dynamos*; they tend to be *busy*, *honest*, *tenacious*, *versatile*, *workmanlike*. They ***prompt***, *hustle*, *beaver away* and *work themselves into the ground*. The *midfield* can be *flooded* or *swamped* by one team (or *con-*

gested by both teams), so that there is *precious little space* there.

Midfield general: The player who *pulls the strings*, the man *at the heart of the action* or *of everything good* the team does. *Midfield generals* are supposed to be admired, but the term may hint at an ego or suggest some imperiousness, so a midfield general may be described less equivocally as *the playmaker*. A **pint-sized** and foreign *midfield general* may invite the designation *little Napoleon*. See also **instrumental**.

Miskicks: There seem to be no gradations of *miskick*: they are invariably *complete miskicks*. *Airshot* is occasionally imported from golf for the instances which really are *complete miskicks*, and *miscue* from snooker when players mishit a *potshot* on goal. More skilled footballers never 'cue' though.

Missile: Can be anything from a coin to a football programme, from a bottle to a pig's head, provided they are thrown by **so-called fans** onto the pitch. *Projectile* is a more pompous alternative but somehow less likely to convey a sense of moral indignation in the commentator.

Mistimed: When managers defend a **tackle** by saying it was *mistimed* and their player is *not that sort of **lad***, you can be pretty sure it was *shocking*.

Mix: Towards the end of games where a side is *striving for the equaliser*, they are sometimes exhorted to get it *into the mix* (or *mixer*), which is a synonym for penalty box: 'Really Sunderland have to get the ball back *into the mixer* if they want to get **something** out of this game'.

Mortgage: Used almost invariably in the past conditional, thankfully for the speaker's financial well-
being: 'I would have *put my mortgage* on Shearer
scoring from the spot there, Clive'. The alternative is
house, but in modern Britain this amounts to the
same thing for most of us.

Mould: There are probably more managers than ever
who were once players, so it is now common to hear,
among older observers and commentators that, for
instance, 'Wycombe are a team very much *in their
manager's mould*'. A footballer who reminds you of a
previous player may be described in such terms too:
'He's in the Ron Yeats *mould*'.

Movement: Teams or players can be characterised by
good *movement* (*movement* is rarely mentioned in
negative statements – see instead **square**, **static**),
that ability to make runs into **space** and *shake your
marker*. It is reserved in general for the *movement* of
players running off the ball. *Moves well* tends to be
combined with *for a big man*, as athleticism goes
without saying otherwise.

Murder: In football, *murder* is not quite as terminal
as you might think: 'We *murdered* them today, but
couldn't quite **kill** them **off**'. Most frequently to be
seen in press conference post-mortems after the opposition's corpse has been miraculously revivified when
it should have been **put away**: 'We *murdered* them in
the second half so for them to go up the other end and
score was a *heart-breaker*'. Football parlance, perhaps
aware of the fatigue to which its metaphors are subject, often gives you an adverb for free, as in 'we
absolutely murdered them' or 'he **completely disappeared**'.

N

Naive: Tends to be accompanied by the adverbs *defensively* or *tactically*. Remarked upon above all when such naiveté is being *ruthlessly **exposed***. The conjunction of these terms suggests that guile and experience are necessary to defenders and managers, while strikers can rely on their ***instincts***. Can still be heard levelled at the *so-called **lesser nations***, especially African teams – unless they have a European manager.

Narrow: Footballing hyperbole inflates a *narrow* or *tight* angle into the superlative: 'Gudjohnsen and Duff combined to ***release*** Hasselbaink, who beat Oakes *from the narrowest of angles*'. But the narrowest of angles would presumably involve a shot from the goal-line, so the phrase is not to be taken too ***literally***.

Need: Many a game is said to *need a goal* by commentators in need of excitement: 'You're right, Mark, what this game really *needs* is a goal'. Generally, games *need a goal* only as long as it's 0-0. They never need additional goals (nor indeed anything else) though some matches simply *cry out* for someone to *put their foot on the ball* or for a bit of ***quality*** in the ***final*** third.

Neon lights: This is what players who try, and fail, with a spectacular or ***audacious*** effort envisage, when they might have had more sensible ***options***. 'I think Eric Young must have seen his name in *neon lights* for a second there. Goal-kick'. *Neon* is not compulsory in this phrase: you can use *bright* or drop the adjective completely.

Nerve: When a penalty-taker is said to have *kept* or *held his nerve*, he is understood to have scored: 'After Pearson was hauled down, Stewart *kept his nerve* from the spot'.

Net: As a verb, equivalent to *score*. The noun is often preceded by *empty* when the goalkeeper has been rounded, although the *net* tends to be quite empty even when protected by goalkeepers (apart from that little kit bag thing they like to put in one corner). Goalscorers *hit* the *back of the net*; hence teams experiencing a goal **drought** cannot *find* the *back of the net*. *Net* becomes *netting* only when you hit its sides.

Net rash: Not a recognised medical condition, but football's colourful way of indicating that a goalkeeper has been picking the ball out of the net too often: 'Ian Walker's in danger of getting *net rash* the way we are playing'.

Neutral: There is no reason why a *neutral* should not also be a **purist**, but *the neutral*, as a rule invoked in the generic singular (although there may actually be as few as one neutral at British matches), tends by contrast to love as many goals as possible. The *neutral* will savour the *comedy defending* that leads to them too: 'It's great fun for the *neutral*, but heart-stopping for both sets of fans'.

New-look: For some reason, football people tend not to say simply *new*. There is instead always talk of a *new-look* **line-up**, a *new-look* backroom team, a *new-look* Ewood Park. Compare **kick-start** instead of *start*.

Nonchalant: The Brazilians are adored for their *non-chalant flicks*, but if the Blackpool number five *dilly-*

dallies at the back he is being 'a bit too *nonchalant* there'.

No-nonsense: A *no-nonsense* midfield is unlikely to **over-elaborate**; a *no-nonsense* referee is usually quick to *reach for his pocket*; a *no-nonsense* defender will put the ball in *Row* **Z**.

Nonsense: Mildly censorious way of talking about **handbags**. *Antics* is another alternative, although this can be used more positively of the practical jokes of **characters** in the **dressing room**.

Not fit: To be distinguished from *unfit* or *struggling for fitness*, in that it refers to moral suitability rather than physical condition. For example, when player A is *not fit to lace the boots of* player B (or *lace the drinks* if player B likes a tipple) a contrast in attitudes and professionalism is made extravagantly obvious. Another instance is *not fit to wear the **shirt***, employed when a player has let down his side with a poor **work-rate**, a fit of petulance or, worst of all, a gesture of defiance to his own fans. An expression that momentarily came to life when an Everton fan ran on to the pitch to offer **lackadaisical** Alex Nyarko his shirt in exchange.

Not the best: Meiosis for 'very bad': 'I'm not saying he meant to hurt anyone but it was *not the best of tackles* and he will see that on the video'. Occasionally a striker's effort on goal is described as *not one of his best* (compare **disappointed**).

Nothing: Often preferred to *nil* north of the border, just as *north of the border* is often preferred to *Scotland* by commentators south of it. Hugh Johns also preferred 'one-*nothing*' during his ITV commentaries of the 1970s, perhaps to avoid the 'one-*nil*' catchphrase of his BBC rival David Coleman. Individual skill can sometimes *conjure* a goal *out of nothing* (compare **nowhere**). Whereas a *nothing ball*, the result of **hit and hope**, is a disappointing end to the move.

Nouveau fan: Not really that common a label, the term mimicking the sort of language such a fan would himself use, while most supporters would come up with blunter names for him. But its Frenchness is apposite, partly because of the enviable success of the French national side or, if you prefer, *les Bleus* (compare **League**) in recent years, and partly because the French language corners the market when it comes to *bourgeois*, *parvenus* and *arrivistes* of different sorts. The middle classes have always gone to football in Britain, and the term is levelled not at them, but at people who, while professing an interest in football, think *Tuscany* when they hear *Villa*, *Rugger* when you say *Brian Moore*, *Good* when they see *Baddiel*.

Nowhere: Whence gifted players come up with chances: 'Kanouté produced a goal from *nowhere* with a stunning strike'. Where players are sometimes going before they are fouled: 'You have to say Scholes was *going nowhere* really until Taylor *needlessly* caught him'.

O

Obscurity: Noun preceded by either *non-league* or *mid-table*.

Occasion: When a manager formulates a *game plan* against certain opposition or *keeps tabs* on a player, he will claim to have had them *watched* on a *number of occasions*, the phrase quietly suggesting that he presides over an outstanding *scouting network*. As an alternative to talking about the *big-match* **atmosphere**, commentators can observe *a real sense of occasion*. Players do not suffer from stage fright but can let the *occasion get to them* in a dauntingly big match. And when Italian *imports* translate themselves in post-match interviews, *occasion* becomes a synonym for *chance*.

Odd goal: 'Thistle won by the *odd goal* in five'. Superfluous, circumlocutory way of saying 3-2, usually to add variety when **rounding up** a series of results. Rarely used for other **scorelines**.

Of age: A phrase emphasising a player's precocious talent. Note how prodigies such as Ian Snodin are invariably described as *only 18 years of age* rather than 'only 18 years old' or 'only 18'. In the same vein commentators can purr over the maturity that can be shown for *one so young*: 'The Doncaster **starlet** has *an old head on young shoulders*'.

Off the pitch: Can be a more telling dimension than *on the pitch*. Frequent in player profiles to warn you that the secrets of a private life are about to be revealed: '*Off the pitch*, Lee likes nothing better than to **relax** with steady girlfriend Alicia over a glass of wine' – it is reassuring to know that he does not do this on the pitch. Often also a convenient way of criticising a player's conduct by inference: 'He's such a polite, pleasant person *off the pitch*'. The two phrases can combine, particularly when there is talk of **well-documented** problems: 'It's been a difficult twelve months *on and off the pitch* but everyone at the club has worked hard and stuck together'.

Office: In one of those phrases which suggest footballers are professionals, just doing a job like the rest of us, defeats are sometimes rationalised as *bad days at the office*. Perhaps a more understandable usage when used of **officials**: 'Paul Jewell complained that nothing happened to referees if they have a string of *bad days at the office*'.

Officials: There are now four of these, known collectively as the *match officials* in club programmes, but it is only the *fourth official* who is habitually called an *official*. The referee presumably is the first *official*, his linesmen, sorry assistant referees, jointly second *officials*, but they are never described as such.

Offside: Always a *trap*, and if ineffective, usually *sprung*, or more plainly, *beaten*. See also *yard*. *Onside* (often abbreviated to *on*) is normally worth talking about only if there is a *suspicion* it was not: 'I think Venison was just *playing* Bright *on* there, Mike'.

Old boy: Although the days when Old Etonians won the FA Cup are behind us, the public school phrase may still be used of players *renewing their **acquaintance*** with former clubs: 'Liverpool *old boy* Robbie Fowler goes back to his old *stamping ground* today'. The term does say something more than merely **former** or *ex*, insofar as it implies a youthful association and some lingering mutual affection. For these reasons, although Leeds was a subsequent former club of his, Fowler would not be described as a 'Leeds old boy'.

Old-fashioned: Sometimes preceded by *good*. Reserved as a rule for the description of **centre-forwards** who have teeth missing and can only head the ball (or goalkeeper). Used also with the nouns **shoulder** *charge, mudbath, cup-tie and free-for-all*.

On the ball: A defunct exhortation, commemorated in the title of some television programmes and in a timeless (and tuneless) anthem at Carrow Road, if City are playing well.

On the night: A phrase that distinguishes a result over one leg from the aggregate score, often in contrast to it: 'Although it only made it 2-1 *on the night*, Speedie *levelled the tie* with a firm right foot shot'; '1-0 to Rangers *on the night* then, but they go out *on aggregate*'. Preferred to 'on the day', even if it was an early kick-off in Vladikavkaz.

On the rebound: The orthodox phrase for a score following an initial save from a penalty but, perhaps surprisingly, seldom used in open play. Players are more likely to **follow up** or hit the net at the *second time of asking*.

One-on-one: A *situation* in which an opposing player bears down on the goalkeeper. The phrase is almost never used for *individual **battles*** elsewhere on the pitch. However, you might hear: 'It was *four-on-two* for a moment in that last Wolves break'.

One-two: If successful almost always *neat* or *quick*; if unsuccessful described as *intended* or **ambitious**.

One-way traffic: The opposite of **end-to-end stuff**. As so often in commentary you are made to notice it has been *one-way traffic* when something happens at the other end: 'It was all *one-way traffic* in this one until Shrewsbury sneaked away to *nick* a last-minute winner'. Even the proverbial **coach and horses** can sometimes be travelling in an unexpected direction.

Only as far as: 'Beasant *clears, only as far as* Brace-well'. In radio commentaries, where this phrase is especially common, the listener will have no idea how far this is. The distance is of no importance, the phrase serving only to indicate that possession has changed hands.

Operate: Generally applied to wide players who can switch flank, as in 'Giggs is now *operating* on the right'. But also common to describe the role of the 1s in a 4-1-2-1-2 – 'Batty is *operating* just in front of the back four'; 'Scholes is *operating* in a *withdrawn role* just behind the front two'.

Opportunism: Off the pitch you would not want to be known for *opportunism*, but strikers may be praised for it: 'The game was heading for a ***stalemate*** when a typical moment of *opportunism* from Garner gave Rovers the points'. An *opportunity* is a synonym for *chance* and may be *taken with both hands*, even by footballers.

Opposite number: Archaic reference, from the days before squad numbers, to an opponent in the corresponding position.

Options: Widely employed to indicate the choices available in open play – 'he had *options* ahead of him but chose to shoot' – and sometimes also at a free kick: 'Redknapp and Anderton are the *options* here'. Players are also excused a *wayward pass* if they had *no options* or *no out-ball*. Perhaps the most standard usage of all is to describe what a manager has available to him if he wants to *make a **change***: 'Asaba, Hartenberger and Bernal: they're the *options*, Alan'.

Organised: *Well-organised* is a common way of saying that a team works hard and gets *behind the ball*, but there is sometimes an element of faint praise: 'George Graham will have them *well-organised* but they are lacking a *spark* in the *final third* at the moment'.

Orthodox: While *recognised* is usually qualified by a negative in football parlance, as in 'not a *recognised* striker', *orthodox* is usually positive in effect. It seems to be employed primarily of defenders: 'They've brought on Barton, a more *orthodox* right-back'. *Unorthodox*, on the other hand, pertains to goalkeepers when *improvising* a clearance.

Out-and-out: As a rule used adjectivally with the noun *striker* to designate a *no-nonsense* centre-forward: 'Ellington is being deployed as an *out-and-out striker* whereas he used to play in a more *withdrawn* role at Bristol Rovers'. More common in modern times with the frequent use of the *lone striker*, *out-and-out* is used to distinguish a player who would always take this role rather than *play in the hole*.

Outfit: Nothing to do with *kits*, but a synonym for team or club, typically coupled with a handy geographical reference: 'It has been a bad week for the Cheshire *outfit*'.

Outlay: Generic term for a manager's expenditure, often with a censorious tone: 'Recent performances failed to justify Hoddle's summer *outlay*'.

Outnumbered: Not used so much when teams are *reduced* to ten men, but to indicate a tactical problem where a side is apparently being *outnumbered in midfield* or, say, a full back unlucky enough to be *playing behind* David Ginola keeps finding himself *outnumbered on the left flank*.

Outrageous: In Britain, it is quite possible to be outraged by skill. Skill is *outrageous* when unexpected or improbable. Dummies in particular may be *outrageous*, whereas bad conduct is never so described but should instead be characterised as *disgraceful*.

Outstretched leg: When a defender pulls off a superb sliding tackle or clearance, the limb that effects it almost becomes amputated from the player in the commentator's eyes: 'Cambridge were saved only by the *outstretched leg* of O'Shea'. Note likewise that decapitation can seem to occur when, in a standard phrase, it is said 'the game was stopped for two minutes after a *clash of heads*'.

Over the top: Denotes a *shocking* tackle (of *the ball* is understood) where the player has deliberately *gone in* with **studs** up in an attempt to injure his opponent.

Over-elaborate: Adjective enlisted whenever a *pretty* passing move has failed or a team has missed an opportunity to **test** the keeper by taking one touch too many. One of those compounds (see also **sky-high**) favoured by football parlance, even when the adjective 'elaborate' would do. An elaborate or intricate move, when it succeeds, will tend to be described as *well-worked*.

Overworked: Referring to keepers and defences under pressure. It is tempting to protest that goalkeepers and defenders are paid (some say overpaid) to *do their **jobs***, but the implication is that they are not being properly *protected* by the rest of the side.

Own goal: *Own goals* tend, like deflections, to be described with sympathy for those who fall victim to them. Often therefore preceded by the adjectives *freak* or *bizarre* even when 'incompetent' or 'stupid' might come more readily to mind. 'Lee Martin's *bizarre own goal* gifted Montpellier a first-half lead'.

P

Pace: Of a player, *pace* can be *blistering, deceptive, searing*. With reference to the **tempo** of the game, teams can *dictate* or *step up* the *pace*. *Pace* may also be *injected* whether by a player himself or by a manager putting him on. The adjective *pacy* is used less than one might think and, if anywhere, in the player profiles of programme notes, but little in spoken discourse.

Pacesetter: A discreet way of suggesting that the leaders early on in the season might be provisional. Often indeed qualified by the adjective *early*: 'Barry Town, the division's *early pacesetters*, came a cropper at Afan Lido on Saturday'. Pacesetters will not necessarily always give way to those who are thought to be able to stay the course, as they do obligingly in athletics. Never say 'pacemaker' in footballing contexts, unless you are a manager joking about the *pressures* of the job.

Parity: A posh way of describing an equaliser, almost invariably with the verb *restored* in the passive voice: '*Parity* was *restored* five minutes later when Cottee sneaked in at the far post to convert a Devonshire cross'.

Park: Teams may be *played off* it or, conversely, they may enjoy a *stroll* in it, but applicable also as a synonym for *pitch*: 'McGrain's the most experienced player on the *park*'. Particularly common in Scottish

parlance, perhaps because of the relative frequency of
Park in Scottish stadium addresses.

Part: Vanquished teams often *play their part* in
games admired by the **neutral**. Commentators indicate that an injury will result in a substitution by saying: 'It looks like Immel will *take no further part*'.
Meanwhile, there are certain things that should have
no part in *the game of football:* for example racist
abuse, or spitting, or any other *disgraceful* **scenes**.
Strangely, these are not counted among football's **cardinal sins**.

Partners: An attacking duo, intent on *poaching* goals
for fun, may be described as *partners in crime*. A pair
of centre-backs will never develop the same frisson of
notoriety, but when they develop a good *understanding* with one another they can be said to *strike up* a
great partnership at the *heart* of the defence.

Part-timers: The fact that a team may be *semi-pro-
fessional* is usually emphasised when they have
sprung or potentially can spring a shock: 'The *part-
timers* from the Faroe Islands are giving Austria a real
fright'. Often the professions of individual players are
referred to, especially if it offers the chance for alliteration: 'The plasterer from Plaistow pounced on a
poor clearance as the Daggers got off to a dream start'.

Passage: Commentators can talk of a *wonderful passage of play*, although the phrase lends itself more to
rugby where there are clear phases of possession.
Teams successful in cup-ties *book their passage* into
the next round.

Patchy: Refers to *form*, and for some reason *away
form* in particular. Bad *home form* tends to be *disappointing, inexplicable, perplexing* or *infuriating*.

Pedigree: The FA Cup commands its own lexicon. For example, those clubs or players who have been lucky enough to taste *cup glory* build up a reputation for their *cup pedigree*. Neither of these nouns sits as happily with 'league'.

Peg: Synonym for *leg*, particularly in the Scottish vernacular.

Penalty: Tends to be *hotly **disputed*** even if the ref had *no hesitation* in *pointing to the spot.* You tend to use the verb *penalise* not as a synonym for *give a penalty* but for less definitive infractions: 'Merk's *penalised* the Blues for dissent by moving the free kick forward'. Instead you may, especially if you are still in Scotland, make a rather laboured reference to the award of a *penalty kick*. See also ***given***, ***spot kick*** and ***stone-cold***.

Per cent: The unit of measure for ***work-rate*** and commitment. If managers want real ***industry*** they ask for 110, 200 or even 1,000 *per cent effort*. ***Fifty-fifties*** are tackles where both players will certainly be expected to give at least 100 *per cent*. *Good percentage play* is an expression perhaps more appropriate in tennis or golf, but it can be used in football to describe a *safety first option* by a defender or cautious tactics in general.

Perfectly good goal: Those who score a *perfectly good goal* do not score at all, for this is the formula when a team has a legitimate strike *ruled out*: 'Middlesbrough deserved the win – especially as they had a *perfectly good* Frank Queudrue *goal* chalked off in the first half'.

Perform: Often employed in the negative to indicate a poor team or individual effort: 'We just didn't *per-*

form at all on the day'. Conversely, players who *per-form* **week in week out** are singled out for praise. An accompanying adverb never seems necessary.

Period: Although extra-time is structured as a match in miniature, it is traditional to refer to its halves as *periods*. Now that the golden or silver goal can terminate extra-time prematurely, *period* in fact turns out to be more apposite than *half*. More generally, teams can be said to enjoy or endure good or bad *periods* in a game, although **spells** is more common in this context.

Pick: At most levels of football, players are *picked* and *dropped* for matches. But once they are good enough to feature in squads on the *international stage*, footballers are more likely to be *selected* and *omitted* – in fact the noun *omission*, coupled with the adjective *notable* or *most notable*, is usually privileged over the verb. As a rule the Anglo-Saxon monosyllables *pick* and *drop* evoke the rudimentary actions of a club manager; their Latinate equivalents, *select* and *omit*, are enlisted to suggest the more sophisticated **thoughts** of an international coach. Another example of the usefully hybrid nature of the English language is the availability of both *get stuck in* and *become involved* to describe a player's entrance into a **brawl**, depending on whether you want to be enthusiastic or euphemistic.

Pick out: In technical mode a reporter may find this verb useful to denote a *pinpoint* pass: 'Jan-Aage Fjortoft finished with **aplomb** after Moncur *picked him out* brilliantly'. A commentator in hyperbole mode, after a **screamer** has just whistled in, may exclaim, as if on behalf of the scorer: '*Pick* that one *out.*' For the second usage, where a quick burst of ventriloquism interrupts the usual impartiality, compare '**Welcome** *to the Premiership*'.

Pick up: If you are unlucky as a player you use this verb with *knock*; if you are lucky as a manager in your *wheeling and dealing* you use it with *bargain*.

Pint-sized: The required footballing synonym for *small* or **diminutive** when you want to find an idiom that is instantly intelligible to the *average football fan*.

Place: A synonym for *away ground*, usually laced with respect: 'This is always a tough *place* to play'.

Play a bit: Understated validation of a good player, seemingly always offered, complete with a little nudge, by the elderly man sitting next to you: 'He can *play a bit*'.

Play host: 'Everton *play host* to Wycombe Wanderers'. A verb, like *entertain* ('Dagenham & Redbridge *entertain* Ipswich') or **welcome**, in the thesaurus of those who relay cup draws to avoid just saying *versus* all the time, particularly on the occasion of the 3rd round of the FA Cup. The interchangeable verbs thereby help to evoke the antiquity and gentility of the FA Cup, even if these courtesy terms are liable to recede once the ceremony of the draw has been completed, since one fan will simply say to another: 'We've *got* Southend away in the fourth round'. Since the advent of multiple televised fixtures, the formalities are rounded off by the elegant 'ties to be played weekend *commencing…*'. Although it must be said that the replacement of the traditional bag by the lottery-inspired box has taken some of the *romance* out of the occasion.

Playing surface: The *pitch*, when you wish to evaluate its condition in more technical terms.

Play-off berth: Perhaps this image is used with the hopeful implication that you may be travelling to a higher division.

Plays his football: 'Mpenza, the Belgian international who *plays his football* in Germany...'. The possessive must always be used in this phrase in which the embedded meaning involves 'work' rather than 'play'.

PLC: What a big football club gets called when unpopular decisions driven by commercial considerations are taken: 'No-one wanted me to leave and I was happy at Sunderland, but *the PLC* had to act'.

Pleasantries: Ironic description of an exchange between opposing players or *dugouts*: 'Phil Thompson swapped a few *pleasantries* with David O'Leary, who was left *fuming* after a two-footed tackle by Gerrard on Jlloyd Samuel'.

Pledge his future: Extravagantly quasi-matrimonial way of saying that a player is signing a new contract of some sort. 'Tomorrow he will be *pledging his future* to the Highbury *outfit*'.

Plum: Always used with *tie* to describe the most *mouthwatering fixture* of the round, which may involve a rare visit of the *big boys*. See also *heavyweight clash*.

Poacher: Although clubs may *poach* a player (especially if Sir Alex Ferguson has *tapped him up* first), this word pertains chiefly to the activity of strikers. Thus a *gamekeeper turned poacher* describes the transformation of a defender into an attacker. The expression would not work so well the other way round (to refer to Dion Dublin, for example, instead of to Paul

Warhurst). But it does fit well with the tendency in football to think of defenders and attackers as different species, the former steady and solid, the latter lurking and predatory. Criminal slang is on the side of the striker who *grabs* a goal or *snatches* a winner. Meanwhile, the poaching activity is reflected again in *brace*, used as a common synonym for 'two goals', and typically with the verb ***bag*** to complete the alliterative and metaphorical effect.

Point fingers: One of the classic phrases (compare *no **disrespect** to*) when a manager says he will not do something and then promptly proceeds to do it: 'I don't want to *point fingers* at any of my players but the defending on the third goal was ***schoolboy stuff***'.

Poised: If a game is 1-1 or even 2-2 at half-time, summarisers tend to call the game *poised*, often *nicely* or *wonderfully* so. Whereas, when the early stages of a game have been *full of **incident***, the game tends to have *all the makings* of an *absolute classic*.

Positives: In defeat, a ***consolation*** is to *take a lot of positives* from your *general play*, if you've given a good ***account*** of yourselves. The curious logic is that *positives* are not taken from a match when you have won it.

Possession: *Enjoyed* by the team who has it and sometimes more remarkable when it has not been *translated* into goals by the team *on top*. *Possession football*, in a set phrase, is played by a team that is passing fluently and ***knocking** it **about***. 'Ball retention' is what rugby fans astray at a football match talk about.

Premiership: Introduced, disgracefully, as if there had been no *top-flight* football in England before the *money men* had their way. Statistical achievements are now that much easier to assert: 'Villa had not beaten Leicester in *Premiership* history'. A neologism lodged so successfully in football consciousness that we forget it has no pedigree. Imported from Scotland where the Premier Division had been formed in 1975-76 (perhaps in recollection of the Auld Alliance with France), it serves as a linguistic symptom of the inflation that has vitiated football now that it has become a business. The foundation of the *Premiership*, and the suggestion that you can be more first than first, dates from about the same time as starred As were first awarded in GCSEs.

Preparation: The standard noun (generally in the singular) to be adopted in the run-up to any big game and particularly before an international tournament, it covers everything from results in recent friendlies to relationships within the *camp*, from penalty practice to the state of the hotel: 'Holland's *preparation* has been far from ideal, and the Saudis will fancy their chances of giving a good *account* of themselves'. It is also possible in these circumstances to exchange opinions and pass on rumours about a squad's *conditioning* if you want to sound more informed.

Pre-season: Often used as a virtual noun these days: 'Keane's *pre-season* was encouraging, which is bad news for the rest of the Premiership'.

Presence: Players can have *presence* in the theatrical sense (especially *in the **dressing room***) but much more common is the euphemism for strong tackling: 'Kamara is making his *presence felt* out there'. 'Kamara is *putting himself about*' is another way of putting it.

Pretty: As a rule used negatively in phrases justi-
fying a pragmatic performance: 'Pilgrims boss Neil
Thompson said: "It wasn't *pretty* but the points are
vital"'. Even without the negative the adjective can
still suggest disparagement, as in the phrase *pretty triangles*. See **ugly**.

Previous: A reduction, as in criminal slang, of *previous convictions*: 'Neill, who has *some previous* for those
who remember his challenge on Carragher, made sure
he took *all of* Bellamy there'.

Price tag: Clubs *place a price tag* on **unsettled** players
which they then *carry* until or even after they are
sold. Serves also as a measure of the **weight** *of expectation* under which a record signing may buckle:
'Collymore *carried* such a big *price tag* into Anfield
that he was never going to succeed there'. You can
almost picture the *price tag* hanging round his neck, a
numerical albatross. The image is well suited to the
commoditisation of contemporary footballers, as they
move from club to club. Similar in kind is the description of an international tournament as a *shop window*
for the participating players. Note also that when a
lower-division chairman claims his **starlet** is *not for
sale at any price*, this effectively marks the start of the
bidding process, in the same way that his *vote of
confidence* would be the beginning of the end for his
manager.

Pride: What teams start *playing for* when well
beaten, especially when their opponents are turning
on the **exhibition stuff**, or when they are playing a
group game of only **academic** *interest*.

Problem: On the pitch, used of injuries – 'I think
Ferguson has a bit of a *problem*, Clive' – or of the damage done by a fast or strong forward, frequently

marked by a superlative phrase like *no end of, whole host of, all sorts of*: 'Salas is causing the England defence *all sorts of problems*'. Also a generic term for incidents in a player's private life: 'Merson's *off-the-field problems* have been **well-documented**'. See **selection headache** for a *nice problem*.

Professional: Managers singing the praises of one of their players can go as far as to call him the *ultimate professional* or can settle for *consummate professional*, often adding for good measure that he displays a *very professional attitude in training*. During a game, anybody seen to be avoiding the **cardinal sins** is praised for *good professional play* (this encompasses the well-known *professional foul*). When the abbreviated form is used, it reflects the insider's perspective more sharply: 'We've got lots of good *honest pros* at this club'; 'He's developing into one of the *senior pros*'.

Progressive: Teams that favour a passing game tend to be praised for their *progressive football*. Never are **Route One** teams criticised for regressive football though.

Prompt: As a verb, it pertains to midfielders who specialise in unspectacular, but not necessarily ineffectual, short passes. Less common in adjectival form, but linesmen can be *prompt* with their flags.

Provider: Strikers who have scored can then *turn provider*: 'Proctor *turned provider* in the ninth minute when his cross was *met* by a Kevin Kyle *blockbuster*'. Should Kyle have *set up* Proctor previously, Proctor could be said to *return the compliment*. All these courtesies were more common before people became interested in **assists**.

Pull on the shirt: A similar general idea to stepping over the **white line**: 'When you *pull on that shirt*, you've got to be ***completely*** *focussed*'; 'When I *pulled on* the Scotland *shirt* I felt a real buzz'. Footballers must *pull* rather than 'put' on *shirts*, which have no buttons, but must not besmirch the ***beautiful game*** by *shirtpulling*.

Punch-up: ***Almighty*** or ***ugly*** are the usual qualifiers, and ***brawl*** the preferred alternative.

Pundit: In Hinduism, a holy man or teacher of wise sayings. In football parlance, a member of the *panel*, just as long as he can tell when his microphone is still running.

Punishment enough: The phrase employed when a player is sent off for a foul in the penalty area: 'Surely the award of the *spot kick* was *punishment enough*'. Can lead on to the complaint that the game has been ***ruined as a spectacle***.

Purist: The unfortunate *purist* only ever makes an appearance at matches that are *not* for him or perhaps her. *Not for the purist* is always used to denote a game that is full of goals. So whereas the ***neutral*** likes to see a *hatful* of goals, the purist seems to be a devotee of *tightness at the back*.

Purpose: *With purpose* is more common than 'purposefully' in football parlance: 'Zenden shot *with purpose*'; 'United have started this half *with real purpose*'. Sustained *purpose* amounts to *urgency*, but this term is usually more conspicuous in football reporting by the *lack* of it, so *purpose* is often employed whenever people seem to be trying.

Put away: Primarily describes chances taken but also used with a bit more viciousness (by analogy with boxing) of the opposition: 'Atletico looked out on

their feet in the last fifteen minutes but we just could-
n't *put them away*'.

Q

Quality: Increasingly common in singular adjective
and noun form and, as in contemporary English more
generally, always understood to be of *good quality*: 'It
was a *quality* delivery'; 'Scholes' finish was *pure quality*'. In the plural, on the other hand, football people
tend to be referring not so much to skill as tenacity or
fortitude: 'We showed all our *battling qualities* out
there in the second half'; 'Graham has tremendous
leadership qualities'.

Queue up: When the defence are caught under-
manned as a cross is *whipped in*, the attackers can be
said to be *queueing up to score*. Generally used, as here,
in the continuous tense.

Quiet: 'Orlygsson was having a *quiet* game out on the
wing, *completely* isolated on the far touchline'. This
does not mean Orlygsson wasn't shouting for the ball,
but that he was making *no impression* on the game.

R

Rap: Tabloid terminology for disciplinary proceedings: 'Shearer to face FIFA *rap*'.

Rattle the bar: Shots may *shave the post* or *remove
paint* from the **woodwork**, but the bar, uniquely,

tends to *rattle*. Sometimes both the strength of a shot and the speed of a subsequent event can be conflated for economy or dramatic effect: 'The bar *was still rattling* from Van Nistelrooy's penalty when referee Bennett blew the final whistle'.

React: Players on their mettle are *first to react*; if not they are *slow to react*, sometimes when it is not clear whether the **situation** necessitated reacting to anything. *Reaction* can commonly be an adjective describing a *save* or a noun standing in its place: 'Great *reaction* from Fox there'. It can also be used to describe the incidence of a recurring injury – 'Duncan suffered a *reaction* in training' – or a *hangover* effect – 'They clearly suffered a *reaction* from their great win at Hibs in the week'. More emphasis may be needed for an act of retaliation: 'It was a silly *over-reaction* from the **lad**'.

Read: Verb used often with the noun **danger**, when an alert goalkeeper or defender makes a telling interception. But more commonly, it is the game itself that is *read*, usually by gnarled defenders or sagacious midfielders. *Reading the game well* means making good anticipatory decisions. Usually this literacy connotes experience – hence 'Rooney *reads the game* well for *one so young*' – or implies that the player in question is past his physical peak. The good *reader* may no longer be a good runner: 'McGrath *reads* the game brilliantly'.

Ready-made replacement: When a substitution is forced on a manager by injury and he has the luxury of making a **straight** *swap*, it is one of the rare moments in football where the stock phrase *in the form* *of* may justifiably be employed: 'Nigel fortunately has a *ready-made replacement, in the form of* Iwan Roberts, to bring on'.

Rearguard: A synonym for *defence*, but 'vanguard' is never used to mean attack.

Recognised: Football's own, rather polite way of saying 'proper' or 'full-time', this adjective should only be used in negative formulations: 'Spurs travel to the Priestfield without a *recognised* striker'; 'The Cobblers now have only one *recognised* centre-half on their books'. See also *orthodox*.

Recognition: When *international honours* are bestowed on you and you win a *full cap*, *recognition* has arrived. This is the economical way by which player profiles announce that a footballer has played for his country. Sometimes used in conjunction with the name of the national team in question – 'Bruce never earned England *recognition*' – though not apparently of those beyond the British Isles. Uncapped players talked up by programme notes may find themselves *on the edge of* or *not far off* international *recognition*.

Recruit: Describing a *recent acquisition*, generally for a few months after he has been recruited. Usually a foreigner – 'Walsall's Portuguese *recruit*' – which means that *import* may serve equally well.

Regular: As a noun preceded by *first-team*; as an adjective precedes *first-team football*. Note also the reference to a team's *regular* strikers or keeper (used less of other positions). The phrase *on a regular basis* conveys the *week in week out* consistency to which all players and coaches aspire: 'Duff's always been quick and *tricky*, but now he's starting to score goals *on a regular basis*'; 'When I'm appearing in the team *on a more regular basis* then I will have *arrived*'. Use this longer phrase in preference to 'regularly' (in the same way as *at this moment in time* should be used rather than 'now', and *of late* instead of 'lately').

Regulation: Generally an indication of straightforward goalkeeping: 'It was a *regulation save*'; 'It came
at *regulation height*'.

Reign: A managerial *spell* or period of *tenure* (though
you seldom hear the latter) becomes a *reign* if at all
successful or of any length (the two criteria tend to be
linked), even though the reigns of English kings and
queens could be both brutish and short: 'John
Rudge's *reign* at Vale Park came to an end after 19
years'. Even the truest-blue scholar of football will
hardly thank us for restating the well known fact:
'Birmingham City did not win once in the *reign of*
Pope John Paul I nor in the course of either of the
conclaves before and after'.

Relax: What teams are sometimes asked to do in
order to *express themselves*: 'In a funny way the first-
leg deficit allowed us to *relax* and I told the players
just to *go out and enjoy themselves*'. **Off the pitch**,
since the abolition of the maximum wage, footballers
admit to *relaxing over a meal and a glass of wine*, not a
skinful of ale on an empty stomach.

Released: In an example of how commentary tends
to praise **quality** *on the ball* ahead of **movement** off
it, a perceptive pass is said to *release* the player it
finds *into space*, even when the run made the pass
possible. Otherwise *released* is the standard term for
what happens to a player when his contract is termi-
nated.

Relegation: A fruitful *zone* also for metaphor and
melodramatic suggestion. Teams facing the *drop* find
themselves in the *relegation zone*. Then, if results fail
to improve, they find themselves *deep* in the *relegation
mire*. They become *locked* in *relegation dogfights* and
scraps. The *spectre* of *relegation looms* or *looks them in*

the eye. They are *all but* down at the point when *sur- vival* becomes only a *mathematical possibility*. In a final *coup de grâce*, they fall through the *relegation trapdoor*. *Finis*.

Representative: In the latter stages of knock-out tournaments, clubs or even countries find themselves increasingly described as *representative* of some larger entity to which they belong, particularly as other *rep- resentatives* fall by the wayside: 'Cameroon are Africa's only *representatives* left'; 'United, England's last remaining Champions League *representative*…'. This usage is not confined to football, but only in football can you read the following: 'FA Cup *surprise package* Farnham Town are alone in *flying the flag for* the Seagrave Haulage Combined Counties League'. See also *advert*.

Respect: It's extremely rare for managers whose teams have had a *wake-up call* to admit to having *underestimated* the opposition. Conversely, coaches of *underdogs* are more than happy to pronounce after a game that they gave the opposition *too much respect*. This may take the form of *standing off* and *letting them play*.

Respectable: 'That goal makes the *scoreline respect- able*'. *Respectability* is a sort of *consolation*.

Restart: The beginning of the second half: 'Albion fell further behind within 35 seconds of the *restart*'. Tends not to be used, as might be supposed, when play resumes after a goal has been scored, nor when extra time begins.

Restraint: Because football is such a physical game, whenever there is *provocation*, any *restraint* shown by players is always *admirable* or *remarkable*: 'After his *howler*, the Finnish stopper showed *remarkable restraint* in ignoring the *provocation* of the idiotic fan'.

Result: Without qualifying adjectives, *result* normally means *win*. Although the implication can be that *something* out of the game is better than nothing: 'Ibrox is a tough place to get a *result*'. When managers say 'it will be an achievement to get *any kind of result* at a *place* like this', they are probably not expecting *floodlight failure* before half-time but implying that their team will get beaten. *Results elsewhere* are what worried benches and fans keep their eye on late in the season, especially if their fate is *out of their hands*. These fans may include *old boys*. 'I always look for their *result* first' is the standard, incontrovertible proof of a player's undying loyalty to the club he has left for a richer one. He may indeed still have *lots of friends* at his former club, even if he prefers the *set-up* at his new one.

Resurrect: Teams can be *crucified* (sometimes *absolutely crucified*) when defeated humiliatingly, but *resurrect* is normally used when an individual player has an opportunity to *kick-start* his fortunes: 'Transfer-listed Geoff Horsfield let two *golden* chances to *resurrect* his City career go begging'.

Return: Destined to be *emotional* if a player or manager coming back to his former club remains on good terms with it (or if Kevin Keegan is involved at all). To be contrasted with *warm welcome*.

Revel: Players or teams can be said to *revel in the conditions*: 'Terry Phelan really seems to be *revelling* in this searing heat in Orlando'. Individual players may also *revel* in an *unfamiliar role*.

Revolving door: Clubs with a rapid turnover in managers are imagined as having one of these: 'There's been a *revolving door* at Blundell Park for the last few years and this *football club* needs some stability'. Some managers, you can imagine, never really get out of the door, let alone into the *hot seat*.

Reward: A goal when scored by a hard-working striker: 'Gary Lund got his *reward* on 75 minutes'. A goal is in general only a *reward* when it is the first or only goal the rewarded player scores. No player, it seems, deserves a *reward* of more than one goal.

Right: Perhaps the classic footballing example occurs when a commentator is enthusing about an exceptional piece of play: 'What a goal! Van Basten had *no right* to score from there'. He of course means to appreciate rather than to invalidate the goal. But when the *right* you do not have becomes *divine*, it always features in admonitory phrases, often warning against complacency of different kinds: 'Forest know that no club has a *divine right* to be playing top-flight football'. Meanwhile, when referees or linesmen are commended by the studio panel or commentators – it has been known to happen – the officials are these days said to *get it right* rather than simply to 'be right'.

Rightly so: A headmasterish afterthought after disciplinary procedures: 'Simeone has been booked for that display of petulance and *rightly so*'. 'He can have *no complaints* about that', summarisers will sometimes echo. The moralising voice may become strident, as in this recent prediction by an England fan recorded in a broadsheet: 'Alpay will be lynched when he gets back to England – and *rightly so*'.

Rise: Perhaps to indicate how easily they have **lat-ched onto** a cross in comparison to a backpedalling defender, forwards are said to *rise*, rather than **climb** (that means something else), often *unchallenged*, at the far post for a floated or hanging cross.

Roar: Noun used to describe the orchestrated en-couragement of the crowd, but perhaps less common nowadays. The *Roker Roar* is no longer; the *Hampden Roar* has been muted by all-seater reform.

Rocket: Occasionally a synonym for **screamer**, but more usually employed as a metaphor for motiva-tional team talks: 'Ian Porterfield seems to have given his players a *real rocket* at half-time'. When referring to individual mentoring, the metaphor becomes even more vivid: 'Darren was *off the pace* earlier in the sea-son, and we had to *put a rocket up him* a few times to get his attitude right'.

Role: 'He's been given a *free role* behind the front two'; 'He has a *roving role* in the midfield'. Sometimes a *role* seems to come with an official permit: 'McMan-aman's got a *licence* to wander'. The term tends to imply an element of creativity, whereas manmarking, for example, is often just a *job*. When they **hang up their boots**, ageing old *pros* may be promised they *still have a role to play at the club* (not merely as lottery-ticket sellers these days, but under the guise of hospi-tality).

Roof: *Nets* and *stadia* are the two places in football where you tend to notice the *roof*. The *roof* can *come off* the latter if the ball *hits the roof* of the former. The metaphor still works even when all four sides of the ground you're commentating at are uncovered. Note also the verb form for an *emphatic* finish: 'Aizlewood *gleefully* roofed that one from five yards out'.

Room: In football, this is more often a verb than a
noun, employed when players away in Europe or on
*international **duty*** share a hotel room – curiously,
even the richest football clubs like to economise in
this way with the premise of building team morale. It
has become the standard form by which a footballer
indicates, without undue sentimentality, that a particular team-mate is also his best mate. 'I always *room*
with Smithy'.

Rooted: Applicable when the goalkeeper makes no
move at all, with *to the spot* left understood: 'Zico's
free kick left Alan Rough *rooted*'.

Rotation: Has a scientific sound to it, especially when
paired with *policy* or *system*: 'Chelsea operate a *squad
rotation system* and Hernan will have to get used to
that'. But the related verb, when conjugated, encour-
ages less professional-sounding alternatives: 'I *rotate*,
you *tinker*, he *chops and changes*'. There was, in the
days of the German Democratic Republic, a club
called *Rotation Berlin*, but it was no doubt the team of
a propeller works or a tank-turret factory.

Round ball: Plenty of sports use a round ball, but
football is usually understood to be *the* definitive
round ball game, when you're contrasting it with the
oval ball game and, say, moving rapidly between
rugby and football results. *Ball* is the standard word
in the general run of play, whereas *football* can suggest a more special kind of relationship: 'You've got to
treat that *football* like a friend'; 'the things Cruyff
could do with a *football* had to be seen to be believed'.
See also ***matchball***.

Round off: A goal which concludes a nice ***passage*** *of
play* or a *neat interchange* of passes, is generally said
to *round off the move*. *Move*, usually a composite of

several passes, should not be confused with *movement*.

Round up: 'Eleanor will now *round up* the rest of the Scottish results'. To the uninitiated, it may sound as though Eleanor will be adding a goal here or there to the totals, but it's a way of summarising the results, once they have, of course, been *classified*.

Route One: The favoured itinerary of the *long ball merchants*. Pejorative in most cases: 'They're just a *Route One*, *hit-and-hope* team'.

Roy of the Rovers: For extra emphasis and alliteration, usually *real Roy of the Rovers stuff*, after the football comic serialisation set in Melchester, as near to 'Manchester' as you can get without alienating Merseyside readers. Chiefly used when a *youth product* makes his mark early in his career, often for his *hometown club* (although you may remember Roy Race was not actually born in Melchester). Roy Hodgson's brief managerial *reign* at Blackburn provoked some new, largely unjustified uses of the phrase. Other references to cartoon characters, also rather obsolescent now, are *Billy Whizz* and *Captain Marvel*. The names of individual players likewise give sub-editors some scope for fairly gratuitous headlines: '*Flash Gordon* fires Canaries towards Europe'; '*Dennis the Menace* breaks Scottish *hearts*'.

Ruined as a spectacle: Tends to be used in postmortems to games where there has been an early sending-off: 'Referee Mike Dean followed the letter of the law but it *ruined* the game *as a spectacle*'.

Rule out: What injuries do to players: 'Owen's hamstring *rules him out* of the midweek clash'. Tempting as it is to picture the hamstring getting a ruler out and putting a line through Owen's name, the usage is so automatic as to be invisible.

Run of play: Locution which necessitates the preposition *against*, used exclusively when a team scores though being outplayed. We thereby infer that an **injustice** has occurred. On local radio, perhaps understandably, the non-regional team always seems to score *very much against the run of play*.

Run riot: Though threatening at times to be interpreted literally since the advent of **hooliganism**, still used figuratively to denote the superiority of one team.

Run the clock down: Opposing teams *waste time* or, more idiomatically and bookably, are guilty of *timewasting*. But your own players would never do that. They merely *run the clock down*. The adjective for them is **cynical**; the adjective for you is **professional**.

Run-in: 'Of the contenders, Arsenal have the trickier *run-in*'. Refers to the fixtures towards and at the end of the season which decide championship, promotion and relegation *issues*. No-one knows exactly when a *run-in* starts.

Running: Like classy racehorses, good teams and players are always *full* of it.

S

Salmon: 'Tony Dennis leapt like a *salmon* for such a small man and Taylor applied the finishing touch'.

The simile is always reserved for headers where the player has *got up well*, often when he is ***pint-sized***. Goalkeepers do not leap in this way, since they are already supposed to be like ***cats***.

Saw it all the way: Another circumlocution (always to be used in this tense) to indicate that a goalkeeper made a routine save: 'It was not a bad effort from Jim Tolmie, but Avramovic *saw it all the way*'.

Scalp: *Scalps* are taken in the Cup by *giant-killing* teams. The metaphors are consistent with one another even if they add up to being a conflation of Amero-Indian history and biblical narrative. Scalps in football are usually *notable*, occasionally *prized*.

Scandinavian: 'The ball fell at Pedersen's feet and the *Scandinavian* needed *no second **invitation*** to ***slot*** it *home*'. Live commentators will remind you where a player is from instead of repeating the name again and again. For some reason, Norwegians, Danes, Swedes and Icelanders, of which there are many in British football, often seem to get called *Scandinavian* players, while Spaniards are not called 'Iberians' or Croatians 'Slavs'. It is probably because they are not exactly sure where Pedersen comes from. *South American* is also useful in case you confuse Bolivia and Venezuela, but Brazilians are more frequently identified as 'Brazilians' than 'South Americans'. Another reason might be that these terms convey certain archetypal characteristics: reliability and steadiness in the case of the Scandinavians as opposed to skill and mischief with the South Americans. The periphrasis is thus likely to surface in place of the player's name when the stereotype is active: 'It was a *glaring* miss from Solano after the *South American* had brilliantly jinked his way into the danger zone'.

Scenes: *Fantastic scenes* is how hyped-up commentators remark on a jubilant crowd exulting in their team's victory. *Disgraceful scenes* is the corresponding phrase when **hooliganism** *rears its ugly head*.

Schoolboy: A standard qualifier for *error* and *defending*. Despite the origins of the term (see **howler**), it tends to mean *abject* rather than particularly **naive**.

Scoreline: Commonly paired with *reflection* and *play*, particularly when England are losing: 'The *scoreline* is not a true *reflection* of the *play*'. *Score* would seem perfectly serviceable, but *scoreline* is often preferred by journalists allergic to monosyllables.

Scrappy: Often when there is no **shape** to either team or to a game itself, it will be called *scrappy*. A *scrappy* goal (but *they all count*) never *lives long in the memory*, or, if you like extravagant understatement which is so popular in football parlance, 'it won't be winning any **goal of the season** awards'.

Scraps: What *predatory* strikers *starved* of **service** are reduced to feeding off: 'Austria's *well-marshalled* defence left Armstrong and Hamilton with only a few *scraps*'.

Screamer: A shot that results in a goal, often qualified as an *absolute screamer*. Presumably derived from the sound that the *howitzer* makes through the air as it flies towards goal. It has been known for commentators, perhaps when they want to emphasise the richness of the **contact**, to drop the 's': 'An absolute *creamer* from Tony Currie there'.

Sea of players: Emphasises a particularly dense *crowd scene*: 'Scholes's shot went through a *sea of players*, hit the far upright and bounced away'. Particularly generous defences have been known to *part like the Red Sea*. A **coach and horses** may be in order.

See: 'Le Tissier *saw* his penalty saved by Crossley'; 'Barry *saw* his goalbound header *cleared off the line* by Kelly'. A little trick of journalistic narrative through which the reporter seems momentarily to collude with the player denied. There is probably no guarantee that the player actually had time to *see* the unsuccessful outcome. If a player beats his man with some skill and impudence, one or two summarisers will on his behalf address the hapless opponent with the mischievous words *see you later*.

See red: In standard English, the phrase for a momentary loss of control. In football, particularly in hurried evening editions or compressed Ceefax prose, the term stretches to embrace not only what happens to players who lose their tempers but what happens to them once the referee loses patience: 'Mikkel Beck *saw red* after his reckless tackle'. A reliteralised idiom, in effect.

Seemingly: Adopted, often with a split infinitive, when hindsight tells you there was a subsequent turnaround in a game: 'Sunderland got two more, from Proctor and Phillips, to *seemingly* put the tie beyond Souness's men'.

Selection headache: Managers with a full complement of players or an *array of talent* at their disposal, traditionally suffer from this ailment. This kind of *headache* is 'a *nice **problem*** to have'. But resist any inclination to *tinker*.

Sell short: Underhit passes, particularly backpasses now that keepers have to kick them, govern this verb: 'The backpass from Beckham *sold* James *well short* but he *spread himself* well'. The usage is comparable with doing one of your team-mates no *favours* or, in a more ironic version, of *rather overestimating his athletic abilities*.

Sent the keeper the wrong way: Another way of saying that a penalty-taker has scored, as though *sending* the keeper (*wrong way* can be understood) itself were a sufficient condition for a goal. Compare *nerve*. Teams can be said to *miss* a penalty even when the goalkeeper saves it.

Servant: Usually in the expression *great servant to the club*. It is impossible to have been a *great servant* for a short period of time. *Great servants* have to be loyal and preferably a bit unspectacular: 'Jason Dodd has been a *great servant* to Southampton'. Tony Adams, on the other hand, though he could be called a *great servant* by most criteria, is *afforded* legendary status for being that bit better. To be an *ambassador*, there usually has to be an element of international *duty*.

Service: Provided by the midfield to the forwards. *Misfiring* strikers are excused when deprived of it: 'Jardel and Grabbi are not to blame. They're getting no *service*'. *Normal service* is resumed when a striker rediscovers his scoring *touch* or a team recovers its form. In the plural, a somewhat archaic way of announcing a purchase: 'We're very pleased to have secured Carl's *services*'. Motorway *service stations*, incidentally, only get mentioned in football when the *tiny minority* of *so-called fans* arrives or if there are *bungs* to be administered by a manager who may on these occasions bring a briefcase rather than a *chequebook*.

Set piece: A *dead-ball* **situation**, whether a free kick or corner (from some players a *long throw* is *as good as a corner*), at which a team can exploit a carefully prepared manoeuvre: 'We've been working on *set pieces* all week'. Sometimes it would seem that all the practice put in on the **training ground** can work to the detriment of the team's all-round play: 'England have only threatened from *set pieces*'.

Settle: May occur in several footballing contexts. Players can *fail to settle* at a new club, usually because their wives do not like Birmingham or on account of language difficulties. When, say after 70 minutes, a team is said to be *settling for a draw*, this is a dignified way of saying that they're not exactly trying their hardest. Finally, a late strike may *settle it*: '**Honours** were even until Kuqi *settled* it in their favour'.

Set-up: A euphemism beloved of new signings when a move earns them a large wage increase, it is supposed to mean the ground, facilities and much else at a club : 'I was just so impressed by the *set-up* at Middlesbrough that I didn't hesitate...'. In its most expansive version, when *facilities* are *second to none*, a recent **acquisition** can praise *the whole set-up from the chairman down to the tea-lady*. Not that there is likely to be a tea-lady these days.

Shape: A polyvalent word which can apply to the team, the act of shooting or the shot itself. Shape is *kept* by good teams and *lost* by disorganised ones: 'I like the *shape* of the team today with the wing backs pushing up to support'. You can describe the act of someone getting his body into a good position to shoot with a reflexive verb: 'Rae controlled the ball, *shaped himself* and hit an unstoppable 30-yard volley past Jasskeläinen'. Meanwhile, the alliterative phrase *shape to shoot* describes the act of feigning a shot:

'Jevons *shaped to shoot* but instead passed low into the penalty area'. Borrowed perhaps from golf, curled **efforts** are often described as having *great shape to* or *on* them.

Sheet: Goalkeepers try always to keep it *clean*. The opposite of a *clean sheet* is *no clean sheet*, for the metaphor is never extended beyond this – *sheets* are not written on or soiled by goalscorers. Though the phrase is used to praise a goalkeeper in particular, managers also can be heard to say more generally after a **bore draw**: 'I'd have liked all three points, but I'm pleased with the *clean sheet*'.

Shepherd: Although *shepherds* – at least in the *One Man and his Dog* version – spend all their time getting sheep *into* pens, in football the phrase is used exclusively for the action whereby a defender *shepherds* the ball *out* of play, usually managing to **block off** an attacker in the process.

Ship goals: When defences are *all at sea*, they are always likely to *ship goals*. *Leak goals* is a close cousin. Broadsheet writers are allowed to refer to *porous* defences.

Shirt: Although socks and shorts are no less distinguishing, this is the favoured metonym: 'Today sees Kilcline's 250th appearance in a Sky Blue *shirt*'. In the plural used to indicate the number of players gathering in offensive or defensive positions: 'Serbia have got plenty of blue *shirts* into the **mix** for this free kick'; 'There are plenty of red *shirts* behind the ball here'.

Shoot on sight: A phrase which once summarised the policy designed to thwart break-outs from Colditz or escape over the Berlin Wall, and which now designates the conduct of players who think the keeper is *dodgy*, or who enjoy the *luxury* of a lead: 'With a two-goal *cushion* the Hornets started to adopt a *shoot on sight policy* and Devlin, Mahon and Fitzgerald all attempted *long-range efforts* that failed to *trouble* Banks'.

Shooting boots: The measure of a striker's form. He can *seem to have lost* them, then he *finds* them, then he *really finds* them. But he certainly needs to *remember* them in the first place: 'Reading might have won comfortably had on-loan striker Lloyd Owusu *remembered* to *put on* his *shooting boots*'. There do not seem to be 'tackling' or 'passing' boots; rather a defender or midfielder may be said to *recapture his form*, to be *back to his best* or *like his old self*.

Shore up: Defences can be *bolstered* at the start of a match (by a player returning after an injury lay-off) and *shored up* in the course of a game (thanks to a substitution).

Shotstopper: Synonym for goalkeeper which emphasises a particular facet of his game (being *good on his line*), usually at the expense of other attributes he might be expected to have. The noun generally crops up in an affirmative phrase which is then quickly qualified: 'Rhys Wilmot has always been a great *shotstopper*, but he does not **command** his area at all and his *kicking* is *woeful*'.

Shoulder: *Old-fashioned* shoulder charges or *barges* are less frequently sighted (or cited) these days. But good *predatory* strikers are always *on the shoulder* of the **last man**. Those nostalgic for **wingers** who had more *guile* and less **pace** than their modern counterparts like to remember how they would *drop their shoulder*, before swaying their hips with a *bodyswerve*.

Shout: Players faced with a decision whether to play
the ball often *need a shout* from one of their team-
mates: 'That's a *soft* corner. Hyypia just *needed* a
shout from Dudek there'. Such is the cosmopolitan
nature of the modern-day Premiership that these
lapses are often ascribed to a *breakdown in communi-
cation*. *Shout* is also a synonym for *appeal* in the context of penalties.

Show: Often used with the adjective *late*, sometimes,
for devotees of Noel Edmonds or Gaye Byrne, with
the adjective doubled up: 'United's *late late show*'.
Teams or their star players can be *late to show*, by
analogy with racehorses, meaning that it was only
towards the end that *class* told: 'A *late show* from
Raúl gave Madrid the points'. A player who *shows too
much* to an opponent yields possession carelessly to
him, while a goalkeeper can also be guilty of committing himself too early: 'Lee Grant *showed* far *too much*
of his inside left post as the resulting shot was
squeezed past him'.

Showboating: To play to the gallery. Like *ballwatching*, always one of the *cardinal sins* that footballers
may commit. Scorned as *unprofessional* whenever and
wherever it is seen.

Sidelined: Synonym for *injured* but often with the
implication that the player will be *out* for the *foreseeable future* or the rest of the season. Such a player will
always be *on* and not, as one might expect, 'behind'
the sidelines.

Siege: When *one-way traffic* gets held up by a stalwart goalkeeper or by a particularly resolute defence,
the metaphor shifts and football becomes a war again
– the goal is *under siege* by the team *encamped* in the
opponent's half. Managers who see their teams regu-

larly under *siege* are subject to a different version of the same metaphor: '*Beleaguered* Glenn Roeder saw West Ham throw away their lead'.

Signing: Noun synonymous with, but more common than, *purchase* or **acquisition** or *buy* or **recruit**. Although players who have **come through** *the ranks* and been at one club all their career will also have had plenty of contracts to sign (from *schoolboy forms* to that final one-year *extension*), *signings* must have come from another club. Indeed, their provenance is often mentioned in the same breath: 'Spurs' Ukrainian *signing* will need some time to *adjust*'; 'The inspired *signing* from Partick *bagged* yet another *brace*'. Sometimes the literal meaning is rendered more visible when, at the risk of sounding like an autograph-hunter, a manager declares himself pleased to have *secured* a player's *signature*, or when a player agrees to *sign on the dotted line* for the interested club.

Silence: So often the *silence* of home fans when their team concedes is *stunned*. Partisan commentators can also describe such silences as *deafening*, with the same kind of ironic intent as those strikers who **wheel away** to cup their ear to the home fans.

Silverware: A synonym for *trophies*, often uttered by players who are lucky enough to have signed for a club with **ambition** while remaining conscious of the dangers of presumptuousness: 'I wanted the chance of some *silverware*. And Celtic have given me that'.

Sink in: Promotion is an achievement which, as a rule, *sinks in* only on the day that the **computer** produces the fixture list for the following season (complete with **big boys**). As in other sports, a triumph of any moment does not *sink in* as long as you are using the verb *to sink in*. Phrases like 'It's yet to *sink in*, Gary' or 'It just hasn't *sunk in* yet, Garth' are a way of fending off tiresome journalists who want your thoughts while the rest of the **lads** are celebrating. By the time a victory does *sink in*, the player has moved on to different vocabulary: 'Obviously it was nice to win the Cup, but we've got to *look forward* now…'.

Sit: What defensive midfielders (*holding players* is the current argot) do in front of the **back four**. The figure conveys at once obstructiveness and immobility. The verb *sit up*, probably more common in the negative, describes the behaviour of the ball as a striker prepares to hit it: 'Although Akinbiyi was in yards of space, it just would not *sit up* for him'.

Sitter: The classic cliché for a *glaring miss*, usually combined with *absolute* or *complete*. Presumably the underlying reference is to the proverbial 'sitting duck'. The word appears first to have been used in cricket around the turn of the century to denote easy catches, but in football it is reserved for errors of strikers, never goalkeepers.

Situation: Football is just full of *situations – deadball situations, dropball situations, play-off situations, must-win situations, unsavoury situations*. The term has prospered to the point of featuring redundantly in some commentaries: 'If Rovers can win this one game, they'll be in a *semi-final situation*'.

Sixes and sevens: Not an expression unique to football (it comes from City of London Livery Companies squabbling over their place in the Lord Mayor's parade), but used specifically in the game for defences in disarray: 'The Blackburn defence was at *sixes and sevens* again on the half-hour **mark**.'

Sixpence: Still defying metrication, the little *sixpence* serves to show either how neatly a player can turn or how accurately he can place a pass: 'Cassells *turned on a sixpence*, beat two men and found the top corner'; 'Armstrong *put it on a sixpence* right into Holmes's path'.

Six-pointer: Seamlessly upgraded in the English game (although Arthur Cox sometimes forgets) from its antecedent *four-pointer*. As if further exaggeration were needed, the phrase is usually amplified: 'Make no mistake, this is a *real six-pointer* if ever there was one'.

Skin: What wingers do to full backs when they are giving them a ***torrid time*** or letting them know they have been *in a **game***: 'Russell *skinned* his defender before *slotting* home'. Similar culinary metaphors involve being *done like a kipper* or *roasted*.

Sky-high: One of those hyphenated phrases *ever-present* in football (compare **kick-start**, **new-look**). Like its opposite *rock-bottom*, used to qualify confidence: 'After the three back-to-back wins, confidence in the *camp* is *sky-high* at the moment'.

Sleep: 'Tottenham *went to sleep* once again *at the back*'. In this example *at the back* seems like a place conducive to rest, as in the cinema or a classroom. Defences can also get *caught napping,* most likely by a quickly taken free kick.

Sleeping giant: Denotes a big, once successful club now dormant in the lower divisions. This *giant* must be a deep sleeper, spending several years out of the ***top flight***, *languishing* in the lower divisions (Wolves, say, in the 1980s and 1990s), before earning the accolade. The image is not applicable on the *international* *stage* where sluggish nations, pre-eminently Spain, should be described as *perennial underachievers*.

Slick: Can be used as an adjective for a good passing surface, as a verb in the same context – 'rain has *slicked* the surface' – or to describe the passing skills of a side who are so good it looks as if rain has *slicked* the surface every week: 'Depor's *slick* passing has to be seen to be believed.'

Slide rule: An adjectival phrase applied to admirably precise, measured or weighted passes. For another example of defunct technology in football, see ***carbon copy***.

Slightest of touches: A superlative called much into action during commentaries: 'The *slightest of touches* took it past the keeper'. Uttered when, for instance, a *glancing header* finds the net, a *cruel **deflection*** wrong-foots the stopper, or a player connects with a cross that has been *whipped in* at pace. When a cross or pass narrowly fails to be converted, we hear that 'it *needed* only *the slightest of touches*'.

Slot: *Slot home* is a verbal phrase that suggests a routine finish. Players can also *slot into* an unfamiliar role as if they had *played there all their lives*.

Slouch: Offers a way of measuring ***pace***, especially in commentary: 'Harewood gave Phil Babb a three-yard start there, and Babb's *no slouch*'.

Smart: Tends to be used of saves which are as a rule more difficult than ***regulation*** but which the keeper is nevertheless expected to make: 'Keelan had to ***react** smartly* to keep out a David Johnson header'. Managers are always wary of facing teams *smarting* from a recent defeat, with *a point to prove*.

Smash-and-grab raid: Adopted to describe a victory where the winning, and usually away, side have won with goals *on the break*: 'Table-topping Norwich crashed to their first defeat in eight games – the victims of a Cardiff *smash-and-grab raid*'. A way of suggesting that *daylight robbery* can occur, even *under the lights*.

Snow: Perhaps used more of Garryowens in rugby, but if a clearance or long through ball has gone very high you may say that it has *snow on it*, even if you are commentating in Guadalajara.

So-called fans: A common way of describing the **hooligan** *element* used by those who wish both to show their contempt for the *tiny minority* and to confirm that not being a proper fan ranks very high among their possible sins. See also **lesser nations**.

Soccer: A noun shunned by commentators who fear they might sound American if they use it too often. Yet, like 'rugger', it's a good old English contraction – in this case of *Association Football*. Alliteration helped the noun survive through the 1980s when there was talk of the '*Soccer Sixes* Tournament' and *soccer stars* helped youngsters with *soccer skills*. But *soccer* sucked when, later, **football** came home.

Soft: Even though there are fewer **hard men** than in bygone days, footballers still don't care for anything *soft*: 'It was a really *soft goal*'; 'Carbone was guilty of another *soft offside*'. This adjective is useful to commentators who wish to criticise while avoiding morally portentous words like 'bad' or 'unforgivable' – which is what *soft* means here.

Solitary: Comes across as more emphatic than 'one' or 'single' in the following examples: 'Blackburn *pip-*

ped United to the title by a *solitary* point'; 'Houston is the *solitary* **survivor** from the 1976 final'; 'Hakan Suker is the *solitary* striker' (although **lone** is preferable in this context).

Something: In football this means *one point*: 'We deserved to get *something* out of the game, even if we weren't expecting to *come away* with a victory'.

Space: Like **width**, a noun much used and appreciated in modern football parlance. *Space* can be measured by the *acre* or the *ocean*: 'Canoville found himself in *acres* of *space* there'. Good passes not only find their *intended targets*, but find them *in space*. *Class* players always seem to manage to *find* or *create* or *make space* for themselves, just as they seem to have more *time on the ball* than lesser mortals: 'Rivaldo *made space* for himself with a *sublime* dummy'.

Spearhead: Denotes the target man who either *ploughs a lone furrow up front* or who provides a *platform* for others to play off: 'Shearer will *spearhead* the attack with Bellamy *playing* just *off* him'. Preferred to the verb *head*, which has other uses, and broadly synonymous with *lead*, except that a striker who *spearheads* the attack, rather than just *leading the line*, is made to sound that bit more potent and dangerous.

Specialist: 'Anderton will have to see a *specialist*'. This is an infallible, economic way of indicating that an injury sustained by a footballer promises to **rule** him **out** for a long while. It is not always necessary to specify what kind of specialist the ailing player has to see, unless it's *a Harley Street specialist*. Injury permitting, players can be *dead-ball specialists*, and teams *draw specialists*.

Speculative: When executed from some distance, shots, and *lobs* in particular it would seem, may be described as *speculative* – whether they result in a goal or not. When they do, the adjective removes some of the acclaim with which a ***long-range effort*** would normally be greeted by suggesting politely there might have been an element of good fortune: 'Ronaldinho's *speculative effort **caught*** England ***cold***'. The noun *speculation* is usually preceded in football talk by *transfer*, a circumstance which will invariably *unsettle* the player in question even if the opportunity is *rebuffed*.

Spell: Interchangeable with ***period***, especially when one team is in the ascendancy: 'Kettering had a *good spell of pressure* on the half hour'. Also reserved for a manager's tenure at a club, especially if he has returned to it: 'Howard Kendall has mixed feelings about his third *spell* at Everton'.

Spice: Any appetising fixture becomes even more so if there is *added spice* caused by ***history*** between the two clubs. Very often the *spice* is not especially piquant: 'The fact that Lee Clark is a lifelong Newcastle fan simply *adds spice* to this North East derby'. Compare ***ironically***.

Spin: *On the spin* is preferred to *in a row*, as in this tautologous piece of writing: 'The London-born hitman *bagged* his fifth goal of the season to send Burnley *spiralling* to their fourth defeat *on the spin*'. Synonyms are *on the bounce*, *back-to-back* and *on the trot*. This last phrase featured in the following curious sentence spotted in a broadsheet: 'Unpredictable Manchester City have now lost seven games *on the trot* and have not won in fifteen'.

Spine: The phrase *good spine* signifies a team blessed with a good goalkeeper, central defender, *ballwinner*

and centre forward: 'There's a good *spine* to the team
with Andy Hessenthaler back in midfield'.

Splinters: What you get if you are *out of favour* and
have been *warming the bench* too often instead of getting *first-team football*.

Spoil the party: Very common in end-of-season football reporting, this is the uncharitable act of teams
with the audacity to draw against or even beat opponents celebrating a feat like promotion or a championship win: 'Norwich nearly *spoilt the party* with an
equalising goal, but Davis **grabbed** a late winner for
the *exultant* champions'.

Spoils: Although the winner traditionally takes all
the *spoils*, in football parlance the metaphor tends to
be used to provide an alternative to *draw*: 'Paul Simp-
son and David Hodgson were happy with *a share of
the spoils* in the **battle** of the *basement boys* at
Brunton Park.'

Sporting: Only in the English language does *sporting*
denote a moral attitude as well as a physical disposi-
tion. It is therefore used sparingly in the British game.
Like tweeds, the term is more common among continentals than among the English whose conduct they
would emulate. Though the likes of *Sporting Lisbon*
borrow an English term, it is a term no English club
has in its title.

Spot: When referees pick up a piece of foul play they
are praised for a good *spot* or are said to be *spot on*.
'Shirtpulling was a *good spot* by Mr Frisk there'. Occasionally the phrase is also used to denote the **vision**
necessary for a good pass. The Big-Ronism was *spot-
ter's badge*.

Spot kick: Alternative to *penalty* which tends to be used only in the singular, mainly in the course of ninety minutes. This is curious given that the *dreaded* penalties or penalty shoot-outs are not really penalising anything (other than the failure of teams to beat one another) and *spot kick* might in this case be more apposite.

Sprawling: Describing a fairly desperate *save* or *stop*: 'The Gillingham keeper made a brilliant 57th-minute *sprawling stop* to fingertip a Tonge free kick *special* round the post.' Used when the commentator or journalist did not think the keeper was going to make it.

Spray: Steven Gerrard qualifies as a person who can *spray* 30-yard passes *at will. Ping* is an alternative. Sometimes the activity can become fairly ineffectual though: 'They're really *spraying it around* and if anything nobody is *putting their foot* on it'.

Spring: The generic noun for a player's ability to *get up* in the air: 'Scholes has such *great spring* for a little man'. With the verb, you can *spring* a *surprise* or the *offside trap* (or both at the same time if you were playing against George Graham's Arsenal).

Squad number: The final ignominy for an *out-of-favour* player is not to be *assigned a squad number*. This way you really can become **anonymous**.

Square: To cross the ball – 'Galvin *squared* to Stapleton' – but also to equalise: 'Romario *squared* two minutes later'. Defences which tend to **step up** can be *caught square* by a **killer ball**.

Square one: While the language of football borrows extensively from other idioms for its own metaphorical purposes, *back to square one* is for once a phrase that has travelled in the other direction. The expression was endowed to the English language by football commentators in the early days of radio when a pitch was divided up into different squares in a plan printed in the *Radio Times* to ease the strain on the imagination of the listeners. *Back to square one* signalled that the ball was with the goalkeeper and another ***passage*** *of play* was about to start. But it seems now to have left the language of football for good. Exasperated managers prefer instead to go back to the *drawing board* or the ***training ground***.

Squirm: Unfortunate goalkeepers allow the ball to *squirm*, often ***agonisingly***, under their bodies or through their hands.

Stab: How to finish from close range: 'After ***good work*** by Pennant, Smith *stabbed* the ball home'. The usage could also hide the suggestion of a *toe-poke*.

Stadium: When clubs move to a new *ground*, they (Bolton, Reading, Sunderland are just a few examples) tend these days to call it a *stadium*, as though this auspicious name were more likely to attract *big nights* of cosmopolitan action. Here the language of football has bifurcated, for fans persist in talking about *football grounds*, while people in suits, like architects and directors, call them *stadia*.

Stalemate: Synonymous with *deadlock*, but, while the latter is *there to be broken*, a *stalemate* is more obdurate or enduring. Indeed, the noun can mean both a result (a draw, obviously) as well as the conditions leading to that result. 'Jenkins has broken the *deadlock* at Vicarage Road, but it's drifting towards a *stalemate* at Prenton Park'. Whereas in chess, from where the term comes, *stalemate* marks the end of the game and the clocks are turned off, the term can be used at any point during the ninety minutes of football.

Stall: Always *set out* by a team **early** *doors* when signalling their intent, usually with hardworking defensive play. The term is used so routinely and with such faint praise that there is no real indication of what is on the *stall*: 'They've come here and they've *set their stall out* and you have to take your hat off to them'.

Stanchion: Corner-frame of the goalpost only ever mentioned when the ball gets stuck in it, which happens on average every twenty years, so that our spelling of this word is provisional. Trevor Brooking, and the keeper who had to dislodge the ball back then, probably know the Hungarian word for it though.

Stand: The verb is a common shorthand in commentary when you wonder whether a goal will be allowed: 'Saha's looking round at the linesman but it will *stand*'; 'They're busy celebrating but it won't *stand*'. The noun of course refers to the *stand* of a football ground, curious in that it used to be the only place to sit. Now that grounds are enclosed on all sides, *stands* are mentioned specifically only when managers are sent off and watch in exile *from the stands*, or when a commentator softens criticism by reminding us that the game is *easy from the stands* or *easy from up here. Grandstand finishes* can happen in football, but the expression always seems homesick for athletics or horse-racing from where it is imported.

Star name: The phrase usually appears in the plural when the players to whom it refers are unlikely to appear – 'Manchester United will be without several

of their *star names* for the ***visit*** of Birmingham' – and
when attendance at a testimonial is being drummed
up: 'Several *star names* had been promised at Sean
O'Driscoll's testimonial'.

Starlet: Typically a young, up-and-coming player
who is good, but not good enough yet to be called a
star. Also sometimes the star player at an ***unfashionable*** club: 'McSporran, the Wycombe *starlet...*'.
Besides, 'the Wycombe Star' sounds uncomfortably
like a local paper.

Static: What defences can be when not reacting to
the movement of the attacking team, while goalkeepers similarly guilty of not moving with sufficient
speed tend to be described as *flat-footed*. *Statuesque* is
an acceptable synonym.

Stature: In football parlance the metaphor *grows in
stature* is often used of young defenders. The time-
frame can be a *game* or a *season*.

Step up: Denotes the activity of a defence which
moves forward in unison to catch an opposing striker
offside: 'The Pompey back four *stepped up* quickly
there again'. *Squeeze up* is a variant. Also used (often
as a noun) to describe the ***gulf in class*** between one
division and another or to indicate the vertigo likely
to be experienced by a player *adjusting* to a higher
division: 'It's a *massive step up* for Zamora from the
Withdean Stadium'. *Step up*, with 'to the plate' understood as in baseball, is applied to anybody who *takes
responsibility*; the locution is particularly apt during
the *dreaded* penalty shoot-out.

Stick: Strikers are often reported to have *stuck it*
(whether the chance or the ball) *away* with ***aplomb***.
The noun refers to the 'post', more often the *back*

stick than the other one. Players can also *get a lot of stick* in the dressing room, although this is used in a playful sense these days for something like a ***dodgy*** haircut. Real criticism would earn you an *earful* or *harsh* ***words***.

Sting: Good, but perhaps rather complacent teams, are *stung into action* by an unexpected goal against them. *Piledrivers*, or *howitzers*, *sting* the hands of the keeper. Though impressive, this is substantially less than what the real things would do to his hands.

Stinker: These days used of referees more often than players, who will have had a *nightmare* if given a ***torrid time*** too often.

Stone-cold: Or *cast-iron* or *nailed on*. Or even *stonewall*. There are lots of different ways of protesting that it was a definite ***penalty***, especially when the referee says it was not.

Stood up tall: For goalkeepers a synonym for ***made himself big***. These idioms work as such only in the past tense.

Stoppage: Used most commonly in the plural or else in the familiar phrase *stoppage time*: 'Roger Milford has added three minutes for *stoppages*'. The *stoppages* in question were not called this while they were happening. Commentators instead wait for a *break in play* or a moment when play is *held up* to read out the ***line-ups*** or turn to their summariser.

Stop-start: Describes *drab* ***affairs*** where there is no rhythm or pattern to the game: 'It was a real *stop-start affair* until the first goal came'. Can also be employed to describe the travails of a player who is injured or out-of-***favour***: 'I had a real *stop-start* first season at the club'. As **kick-start** is preferred to 'relaunch', so *stop-start* is preferred to 'interrupted'.

Storm: The figurative *storms* a team *weathers* (*storms* are never mentioned unless they are *weathered*) tend to be *early*, whereas *scares* can occur either early or late in a game. Conversely, the adjective *storming* tends to be reserved for *second half comebacks* or **passages** *of play* where teams *up the **tempo***.

Straight: A *straight red* is distinct from a red which is the product of two *yellows*. When a player comes on as a substitute for someone in the same position, it is unfailingly hailed as a *straight swap*. But, unlike the Panini stickers which feature them, footballers tend to be *exchanged* rather than *swapped* in the transfer market: 'Blinker goes to Celtic in a cash-plus-player *exchange* deal'.

Stranded: The unfortunate fate of keepers who race from their line or come for crosses, only to see the ball go past them into the *unguarded **net***: 'Seven minutes later Malbranque *turned provider* with a penetrating forward pass that Saha slipped past the *stranded* Seaman'.

Strength: Common in two phrases. Teams are invariably *at full strength* if they have no injuries. *Strength in depth* is the magical property deemed necessary to succeed in the days of squad **rotation** and fixture *pile-ups*. It is the stumbling block for clubs who merely have a good team but are not so unfair as to keep in their own reserves personnel who could *walk into* another club's starting **eleven**.

Stride: The unit of measure for an improving side: 'As Wales prepare for the **lottery** of the play-offs, coach Mark Hughes reflected yesterday on the *strides* his team have made over the last two years'. These strides are often *great* or *massive*.

String: When a goalkeeper is *kept busy*, he may need to *pull off a string* of good or even *stunning* saves. *Influential* players, especially **midfield generals** if they don't mind mixing metaphors, *pull the strings*.

Strip: What footballers wear, or used to. *Strips* are being supplanted by *kits*. Until recently, at least according to the specifications noted in football annuals, a *strip* included *jerseys* and *stockings*, rather than shirts and socks. Substitutes are told to *strip off* by the manager. They don't need to be told that this means only the tracksuit.

Stroke of half-time: Goals which go in after about 45 minutes are, emphatically and precisely, scored *on the stroke of half-time*, even if half-time can be announced only by the referee's whistle.

Strong: Managers trying *kidology* will often demand a *strong referee* for a game *in the lion's den* (which sometimes will actually be Millwall's). S*trong hand* is a specific expression used when the keeper makes a save from a fierce shot if he would normally be expected only to **get a hand to it** as it passed by him.

Studs: In **almighty** *scrambles*, the *studs* tend to **fly** – indeed the image can be used in a wider sense to describe a game where the tackles become **X-rated**: 'After the nonsense involving Sammy Nelson, the *studs* began to *fly* all over the **park**'. If Sir Alex Ferguson's *hairdryer treatment* does not work (see **teacups**), *studs* can even *fly* in the dressing room. *Studs up* can describe any robust challenge, but particularly one where a player has *gone **over the top***. In a similar usage, a player can be said to *show his studs*

(in the direction of a player's backside rather than to
the fourth *official*).

Stuff: A word that appears many times in this dic-
tionary. Its most basic meaning tends to be *football* as
in *great stuff, lovely stuff*. The past participle of the
verb, on the other hand, is used when you have not
played so well and been soundly beaten. Curiously,
managers whose teams have been *stuffed* can confess
to being *gutted*.

Style: Invariably *turned on*, whenever a team is playing *exhibition stuff*. Managers like to think they can
instil a certain *style of play* in their charges. Commentators meanwhile like to observe a *contrast in styles* if
a British team is playing a *technically* accomplished
foreign side. Compare *way*.

Substitution: Should a substitute score or perhaps
play a conspicuous part in a goal, the *substitution*
turns out to be *inspired*. *Last throw of the dice* is the
standard rhetorical description of a manager's final
substitution, even if he can make further tactical
changes. See also *super-sub*.

Suck in: A classic cliché employed more sparingly
nowadays: 'For all the attempts of the Feethams
faithful to *suck the ball in*, it was a poor display'. But
you can still talk about teams being *sucked into* the
relegation zone.

Super-sub: A phrase which first seemed to come into
vogue for the comet that was David Fairclough; now
said routinely of any player who *climbs off the bench*
to score, usually without the implication, once promoted by Fairclough and other *super-subs* of the
1970s, that they were much less effective if included
in the *starting eleven*.

Surprise package: Always a nice surprise – every year there seems to be at least one team in each division who are seen to be exceeding expectations over a season: 'In the first half Nigel Worthington's men were outplayed by the First Division's *surprise package* Wigan'.

Survival: *Survival* would seem to be a modest ambition, a basic *sine qua non*, but, in football parlance, the term again carries its own implicit cargo: *survival* here means 'not being relegated'. *Staying alive* in the cup may be merely a distraction in these circumstances: 'It's nice to be in the hat for the fifth round, but we all know *survival* is the priority here'. Which translates as: 'I can't believe we're still in this cup, because I get sacked if we go down'. *Safety* is a slightly less emotive term. Italians talk of *la salvezza* or salvation in this context.

Survivor: Overblown expression, particularly in the light of real disasters such as the Munich air crash, to indicate a player who is still at a club where ***honours*** were won at an earlier time: 'Tony Adams is the only *survivor* of that double-winning side'. After the death of Diana, Princess of Wales, an edict went to the commentators of the first match to be played (Bradford City v Sunderland) informing them to be careful not to say 'the shot went straight into the wall' or to talk of Phillips' 'killer instinct'. *Sudden death*, however, remains the potentially insensitive description of what happens if the first five penalties of a shoot-out have been taken inconclusively.

Sweet: An adjective primarily used with *volley* to indicate a particularly aesthetic ***contact***, but can be used of any shot or pass. An especially *sweet volley* becomes *sublime*.

Switch: When wingers change sides (*flanks* that is, not teams), they *switch* from right to left or *vice versa*. An ability to *switch the play* and **spray** a pass *into space*, often with **vision**, is the hallmark of a *creative* footballer. *Half-time* is sometimes referred to as the *switch* (when teams change ends): 'Mali will want to make a **change**, I'll wager, but not till after the *switch*'.

Swoop: Adopted when a team moves to complete a quick transfer (or even when they don't). The verb may be combined with the nickname of the club doing the *swooping* to create a comically literal effect: 'The Robins have *swooped in* on Shelton' or 'Grass-hoppers *swoop* for Littbarski'. Like the term **capture**, also widely used for transfer **acquisitions**, this termi-nology perhaps originated in a period before football agents became all-powerful.

System: Most common way of referring to the for-mation a team uses. For example, it may *abandon* a *sweeper system* to go to an **orthodox** back four. In recent years, we also find mention of *squad systems* or **rotation** *systems* which managers operate when their teams are still in several competitions. Scouts always seem to be employed as part of a *scouting system* (which may simply mean Dave Sexton working part-time).

T

Tackle: Good *tackles* should be described as *crunch-ing, robust, rumbustious* or (particularly if a continen-tal referee should award a free kick as a result) *British* – in all the above cases you may roll the 'r' in an attempt at onomatopoeia. With weak *tackles*, some of the available adjectives or adjectival phrases are: *flimsy, spineless, pathetic excuse for a*. If the *tackle* is illegal but thought to have been a **genuine** *attempt* to play the ball, it is described as *not malicious* or **mistimed** (as opposed to *late*, which indicates a degree of malice aforethought). If the *tackle* is really bad, it can produce euphemisms such as *poor, over-robust, scything, not the best of*, or provoke condemnation as *appalling, shocking, disgraceful*. The *sliding tackle* is perhaps the only type of tackle which can have some sort of objective existence. Note that the act of *tackling back* does not necessarily involve actual *tackling*, being used as much in the sense of attacking players getting themselves *behind the ball* when the other side has it. See also **challenge**.

Take each game as it comes: One of the select group of clichés, almost on a par with *sick as a parrot*, that is seldom resorted to by anybody in the game without the qualification that it is the *old cliché*. A similar idea is: 'I can promise you we are not *looking past* our next league game on Saturday against Stockport'.

Take the result: The obligatory post-match interview throws up some formulae of its own. When managers or players profess to be satisfied with a result which, like a slim first-leg lead or a draw, is not obviously satisfying, the standard method for so doing consists of hypothetically *taking* that same result, had it been *offered* before the match: 'The lads are not exactly dancing on the ceiling, but if you'd *offered* us the point before today's game, we'd have *taken* it'. A harmless surmise, but not to be made by anyone with a match-fixing case pending.

Talismanic: More common in adjectival form than as a noun. Pertains usually to a striker with a habit of scoring important goals, and also to any player who can *turn a match*.

Talking point: Tends to be *major*, and in the era of punditry is filed away for discussion *after the game*. But at half- or full-time a commentator will often proudly hand over to the studio panel with words such as 'plenty of *talking points* there', as though he has been responsible for making their job easier.

Target: Strikers both are the *target* – 'we need a *target-man* in the team, *in the **mould** of* Mark Falco' – and are expected to hit it. But *target* is used most commonly in football parlance when it is missed: 'From that position, you've really got to *hit the target* – Tarantini should have made the keeper work there'.

Teacups: Describes a fracas which takes place inside the dressing room, when too many *harsh **words*** have been said and the crockery starts to fly. The *hairdryer* treatment is a recent alternative. Whereas a ***rocket*** is a perfectly acceptable half-time device.

Team affairs: Phrase only to be used during inter-regna when the ***caretaker**-manager* presides. Almost archetypally: 'David Pleat takes charge of *team affairs* until a new manager can be found'. Interesting in that the new manager would not normally be expected to run the ***PLC*** as well as *team affairs*.

Technical: Particularly prevalent in the upper eche-lons of European and international football. Teams whose individual players are blessed with all the req-uisite skills (they have *great technique*) are *technically* accomplished. Sometimes praise in these terms barely camouflages the suspicion that a team may not be the sum of its parts. Or the *technical* merits of a team may implicitly draw you to its temperamental deficiencies: 'The Croats are *technically* very gifted, but they don't seem to have the stomach for a fight'. Nevertheless, the recently invented dotted lines that restrict the touchline movement of agitated managers have been dignified by the term *technical area*, evidence that the adjective continues to live and thrive beyond suspicion. Note also another adverbial usage meaning 'theoretically': '*Technically*, that has to *go down* as a chance', the implication being that nobody could have been expected to score.

Telegraph: When a player *telegraphs the pass* – that is, he betrays his intentions far too obviously to the opposition – the telegraphy in question is presumably the semaphore signalling of old, rather than the more recent and familiar tapping of keys which does not involve overt signalling of intention.

Tempers: Invariably *fray*.

Tempo: The pace at which the team as a *collective unit* is said to play. Usually English teams are exhorted to *up the tempo* and to play with *more* or *higher tempo*. More occasionally you can pause to admire the *lovely tempo* or *samba rhythm* of more patient *build-up* play.

Tempting: Describes crosses, with the understanding that it is the striker who is *tempted* to *apply* a *finishing touch*, though there may be circumstances in which a keeper is *tempted* to leave his line for a cross he cannot reach. It is more usual on these occasions to describe the cross as *teasing*.

Terraces: Once, when stadiums consisted largely of *terraces*, an innocuous synonym for a football ground but, now that all-seaters are the norm, usually

invoked as implicit proof of the loyalty and longevity
of a football fan: 'I stood on the *terraces* of the Gallow-
gate back then…'. Fathers (and any shoulders onto
which a child may have been lifted or rolled-up newspapers which may have been urinated through)
should be mentioned in these cases too. Politicians
are particularly fond of mentioning the *terraces* they
helped to destroy.

Terrier: Describes energetic midfield players. Perhaps it is our imagination but the phrase often seems
to be used of redheads like Alan Ball, Billy Bremner
and Paul Scholes.

Territory: Employed much less than in rugby,
although occasionally you hear of teams being unable
to *translate* their *territorial advantage* into goals.
But one usage that is very common occurs if a free
kick is conceded 20 to 25 yards from goal: 'This
is Neil Clement *territory*, Ron'. *Country* is available
too, possibly with a twist of irony in international
matches.

Terrorise: Unchecked by the events of 9/11, centre-
forwards (usually *bustling* ones, good in the air) continue to *terrorise* defenders, while wingers tend
merely to *embarrass* their ***opposite numbers***.

Test: Verb which in recent usage means to submit to
a *fitness test* – 'Coventry *test* Jenkinson and Light-
bourne…' – but otherwise traditionally applied to goalkeepers: 'Cascarino *tested* the keeper from 25 yards'.
It's always a *test* the keeper seems to pass.

Textbook: *Textbook* appears as an adjective in places,
most commonly when a *textbook finish* results in a
goal. It is difficult to imagine a football *textbook* or lexicon finding many readers.

Thank: When a keeper has played better than his team and *got them out of jail*, the construction is usually as follows: 'Spurs have Thorstvedt *to thank* for a *share of the* **spoils**'.

The: A few exalted clubs enjoy the privilege of a definite article before their names – *The Arsenal, The Villa, The Albion* (*Th'Albion* in local vernacular)*, The Wednesday* (their proud name till 1929). Teams known habitually by a plural may also be called *The Spurs* or *The Wolves*, but, in general, the article should be omitted. When someone says something like 'I love Stoke', confusion can occur (as well as surprise), for do they mean City or city? Italian averts potential confusion by insisting on the definite article when you're talking about a team which is or could be a place (hence *La Roma, Il Lecce*), but English allays it by making the subject plural, hence 'Liverpool are rich', 'Newcastle were lucky'. There is no surer way of betraying ignorance of football than that of using a singular instead. But there is an exception: when, after the success of the Euro '96 song *Football's Coming Home*, fans adopted this tune for their own purposes, the metre forced the plural to become singular. Hence: 'We're going up, we're going up, *City's* going up'.

Theatrical: Awed commentators, delighted to have been chosen for a *big European night* ahead of their colleague left behind at Oakwell, refer to big, historic football grounds as *theatres*. But the adjective *theatrical* in the mouths of the same commentators is unfailingly, puritanically pejorative. *Theatrical* equals inauthentic, unconvincing, histrionic: 'Maric took a *theatrical* tumble, but the ref **waved** it **away**'. References to *Hollywood* often follow, an obvious dive earning a remark like: 'that won't be *winning any Oscars*' or 'that was *pure Hollywood*'. The *Theatre of Dreams* is

of course Old Trafford, but this title sounds manu-
factured, no doubt dreamed up by some marketing
genius. Conversely, *drama* and *dramatic*, used especially of *starts* and *finishes*, are never used self-consciously: 'What *drama* here in the final minutes as
Barnsley score again'.

Thoughts: International managers are perceived to
be more thoughtful than others, for players with a
chance of international **recognition** always enter
their *thoughts*. 'Scott Parker is certain to be in Sven's
thoughts'. **Domestic** managers are more likely to have
prosaic *plans*, usually mentioned with negative con-
sequences: 'I'm sorry for the *lad*. But Andy Todd is
not part of our *plans*'.

Thrash: Good *thrashings*, *thumpings* or *hidings* can
all still be administered on the football pitch, despite
the fact that corporal punishment is no longer per-
mitted, even in public schools. Note a celebrated
Nordic variant: 'Your boys took *one helluva beating*'.
Once players *slap in* a transfer request, a deal on a
new contract is then *thrashed out*.

Throw men forward: Urgent, desperate teams *throwing caution to the wind*, towards the end of matches
which are slipping out of their grasp, do so by *throwing men forward*. The projected men in question are
usually more reticent midfielders and sedentary
defenders, though goalkeepers are known to *come up*
for a final set piece. The idiom modulates slightly
should the opposition *go up the other end and score* in
these circumstances. Then the unfortunate team is
said to be guilty of having *committed too many players
forward*.

Time: Since *extra-time* is specifically the half hour
appended to unresolved cup ties, the time added on to

the ninety minutes is ingeniously known as *time added on*. It is not usual to talk about 'additional time', but it is possible to say 'there will be three *additional minutes*', particularly since the introduction of the *fourth **official**'s* board. *Time added on* may also be known as *injury time* or **stoppage** *time* as opposed to *proper time*. Good players will *time* a run *to perfection* (never 'perfectly'), while the adverb *timely* is always combined with *interception*, or more occasionally **intervention**. Finally, it is a miracle how some footballers always seem to have *time on the ball*.

Today's evidence: 'On *today's evidence* they will be really struggling come the end of the season'; 'On *today's evidence* they really need added firepower up front'. Means 'after this game' but helps to lend to punditry a forensic dimension.

Tone: The *tone* of a game is often *set* by a *crunching* **tackle** or some **afters**.

Too good to go down: Commentators sensibly eschew the words 'good' and 'bad' in general. But a few clubs in the past were considered *too good to go down*. When they did duly go down, the lucky ones to become **yo-yos**, they left this phrase soaked in hubris. You cannot now venture it without an ironic smile. No-one seems ever to have said that a team was 'too bad to go up'. Maybe this phrase lacks the assonance and alliteration of the other, or perhaps it would just be bad manners to say so.

Top-flight: 'This is Pearce's fifteenth season in *top-flight* football'. Usefully bridges the self-invented transition between the ***Premiership*** and the old First Division, or **spells** a player has had in the highest divisions abroad.

Torrid time: Experienced particularly by weak full backs faced by the *mazy runs* of a winger: 'Giggs was giving young Parnaby a *torrid time* down the left flank'.

Total football: There may be some arguments about the derivation of the phrase (although it will always be associated with the great Dutch sides of the early 1970s), but in live commentary it has now become devalued and is used rather lazily whenever a centre-half makes an unexpected *foray*, or someone *pops up* in an unfamiliar position: 'Just look where Lundekvam has ended up in that move. *Total football* from the Saints'.

Track: Can describe the process of marking, especially for forward or midfield players: 'Juninho failed to *track back* and Armstrong took full advantage'. In another usage, managers *track* players, usually for *some time*, with a view to making an offer if they become available.

Tracksuit manager: Denotes not only the choice of clothing favoured by such managers, but also an attitude to the game. You can expect a *tracksuit manager* to have a *hands-on* approach, to love working (*day in day out*) with the players on the **training ground**, and to be having a dispute with his chairman. See also **week in week out**.

Trade: Adopted in connection with the idea of professionalism being a virtue: players *learn* their trade, then *know* their trade, and only in their autumn years *ply* their trade.

Trademark: Used adjectivally in preference to 'characteristic' or 'typical': 'Guppy swung in a *trademark* cross'. Employed also, probably in descending order

of frequency, of free kicks, runs, dribbles, and shim-
mies.

Tradition: 'This is a club with a great *tradition*'.
Likely to be said fondly by the new manager of a club
not faring particularly well in the present, such as
Blackpool or Wanderers (if they still exist). Some
clubs have a good *cup tradition*. Indeed, the FA Cup
in particular attracts all things *traditional*, above all
the *traditional* cup-final anthem *Abide With Me*, the
traditional singing of which is by *tradition* useless.
The adjective surfaces sometimes when team *colours* are described – 'West Ham are playing in their
traditional claret and blue' – and is particularly common if stripes feature – 'Huddersfield, in their *traditional* blue and white stripes'. There seems to be
something inherently *traditional* or *familiar* about
stripes to the English footballing psyche, perhaps
because nearly all the teams that play in stripes
were more successful and prominent in the distant
past.

Trail: Synonym for 'is losing', usually if the team in
question is at least two goals down. The term *trailing
leg* is used by partisan commentators to suggest that
contact was made accidentally rather than because
the player *left his foot in*.

Training ground: 'That's one from the *training
ground*' is a standard phrase that greets a *well-worked*
or perhaps slightly ingenious free kick. For extra
emphasis, the phrase *straight off* or *from* is used, to
confirm just how well the move has translated itself
to a real game: 'Tony Carrs scored the goal of his life
straight off the *training ground* and left beaten keeper
Kevin Dearden stunned'. Players will sometimes corroborate praise for a team-mate by remarking tantalisingly: 'you should see the things he does *in training*'.

This is particularly true of strikers who knock chances in *for fun* on the *training ground*.

Transfer list: Players are *placed* on this list or may be described as *transfer-listed*, even though the list in question seems to be imaginary and certainly not available on the internet.

Travelling army: Any *set* of away fans tends to be called a *travelling army*. But although football fans can be violent and destructive, here the image conveys no menace. Indeed, the *Tartan Army*, Scotland's merry band of fans, is always praised for its pacifism and good cheer when it's not smashing up the goalposts at **Wembley**.

Travels: Perhaps the commonest way of saying *away from home*, especially in the special pleading of managers' programme notes: 'After so many near misses *on our travels* this season, it was nice that everything came right for us at the Riverside'. *On the road* is a variant, even in these days of domestic airflights.

Treatment: One of those words that can have opposite meanings depending on the context. Injured players receive *treatment* from the physio, so that *treatment-table* or *treatment-room* become metonymical: 'The Goodison *treatment-room* is full at the moment, with Ferguson and Gravesen **doubtful**'. But sometimes the reason players take knocks is the *treatment* meted out to them by opponents: 'Young Ronaldo has been on the receiving end of some heavy *treatment* from Kishishev all afternoon'.

Trenches: Imagined in conditional phrases as the location par excellence for commitment and stamina, *the trenches* relativise the talents of certain players not known for *digging deep*: 'You wouldn't want Di Canio *in the trenches* with you'. But note going **over the top** means something else in football.

Trickle: A verb to describe the progress of shots where the striker did not **get hold** *of it*: these usually *trickle harmlessly* to the keeper, but sometimes **agonisingly** *wide* or *over the line*.

Tricky: The favoured adjective for *dribbling* **wingers** or for those away ties, usually against lower opposition, which are a *potential* **banana skin**. An away **date** with one of the **big boys** would be called *daunting* or *difficult* rather than *tricky*.

Troop: The verb to describe the ambulation back to the dressing room of a player who has **seen red** or a team losing at half-time: 'The Mariners *trooped* back to their dressing room no doubt expecting a **rocket** from Alan Buckley'.

Trouble: When you have given a penalty away, an alternative to having your *misery* **compounded** by a *yellow card* is to be booked *for your trouble*: 'Evans was *booked for his trouble* and Bruce Dyer added insult to injury by firing the penalty low past keeper Paston's right hand'. In a classic cliché, an inaccurate pass *plays* one's team-mate *into trouble*. *Trouble* is also used with various parts of the anatomy to indicate an injury that *forces a player off* or *continues to keep him out*. It is never quite clear when *groin trouble* becomes a *groin* **problem**.

Trump card: Considering how much time footballers spend in card schools, this metaphor for the best player in a manager's hand is not perhaps as prevalent as you might expect. The use of *ace*, whether up sleeves or not, as a synonym for *striker* is also fairly rare: 'The Peel Park *ace* stole in to add another to his season's tally'.

Trusty: Indicates a player's preferred foot and, as so often, used more of left than right: 'Fowler swung his *trusty* left boot and Howard never saw it'.

Tumbling: How players are *sent* by over-robust **tackles**. Strangely, nobody ever seems to be sent *tumbling* by fair **challenges**; in these cases, they are more likely to be *outmuscled*.

Turn up: 'We just didn't *turn up* first half and were lucky to go in one-down'. Commentators fond of emphasising the inconsistency of a team will say 'it depends which Chelsea *turns up*'. *Show up* is an alternative. Or this image may be reinforced by a literary allusion – 'Our performances this year have been a bit *Jekyll and Hyde*' – a rather mundane adoption of the syndrome.

Turning point: All matches require (and all commentators seek) *a*, or better still *the, turning point*. They are conjectural and numerous at different points throughout a match – 'That *could prove* to be the *turning point*' – before you settle on a single one at the end: 'The *turning point* in this one was without doubt Wouters' shoulder on Gascoigne'.

Two feet: 'He's got *two feet*'. What might seem a minimal requirement for a footballer is actually a considerable virtue, as players with *two feet* can use either effectively. For added emphasis say *two great feet*. Mind you, a *two-footed challenge* is not so clever, and these days usually merits a **straight** red.

Two minds: Not nearly as commendable as **two feet**. Defenders who get *caught in two minds* – for example, between a backpass or a clearance to *Row* **Z** – usually pay for it.

U

Ugly: Can qualify *tackle* or **incident**, but, with increasing frequency, it surfaces when a manager takes delight in having eked out a result with a poor performance: 'Sometimes you have to win *ugly* and we certainly had to do that today'. (Football managers are particularly known for preferring adjectives to adverbs, as in the now canonical *the boys done great*). If you are Ian Holloway you can extend the idea into the metaphor of pulling a slapper in a nightclub. Another way of putting it is *not* **pretty**.

Unbeaten: Always combined with *run* (whereas rarely do you see 'losing runs', rather *losing sequences*). Alternatively to be used as a complement, when teams *go* a certain number of games *unbeaten*.

Under: To *get it* or *bring it under* means to have **dealt with** an overhit pass or bobbling ball. *Control* is always understood.

Under the noses of: When players are signed in a deal which may seem more scheming than **audacious**: 'Forlan was signed *under the noses of* Middlesbrough'.

Underdogs: Always *plucky* or *valiant* if they lose by less than three goals. Managers playing *mind-games* often aver that their team must **go down** *as*, or *be considered*, the *underdogs*.

Underline: Often used without a direct object: 'Werder *underlined* why they are touted as Champions League dark horses with a 2-0 win'. Good young players seem to *underline their potential* with *eye-catching* performances.

Understudy: This noun spends most of its time in the realm of goalkeeping, where it is obvious that one particular player prevails at the expense of another: 'For so long the *understudy* to Grobbelaar, Bolder has decided to get *first-team football* at the Valley'. Other *theatrical* terms used in football include *curtain-raiser* (the *traditional* one in England being the Community, once the Charity, Shield), *cameo* and *performer* (as in 'useful *performer* on his day'). But when Graeme Souness *makes overtures* to a potential new signing he will not be humming the opening bars of *The Thieving Magpie*.

Undisclosed: A standard adjective when a transfer fee is not in the public domain, although often qualified by the phrase *thought to be in the region of*.

Unfancied: Adjective for teams that constitute a *surprise package*. *Unfancied* is not to be used in circumstances when it happens to be right not to fancy a team. You will rarely hear: '*Unfancied* Halifax duly lost by a hatful...'. The adjective *fancy* arouses great suspicion in football where *Fancy Dans* are not popular *in the trenches*, and complacent or *over-elaborate* teams are warned to cut out *the fancy stuff*. But note the growing use of the verb where a manager confesses he has always *fancied* a player, meaning that he *rates* his exceptional talent rather than coveting anything else about him.

Unfashionable: A polite way of saying 'unsuccessful', though the epithet can be used to highlight the

current achievements of a club that is not traditionally in the running for **silverware**: 'Curbishley has
worked wonders at *unfashionable* Charlton'.

Unforced error: Rare in football, certainly in comparison to other sports, but occasionally used of a
misplaced clearance or backpass by tennis commentators earning a few bob over the winter at football
matches.

Unnoticed: Strikers can *steal in*, especially at the
*back **stick***, *unnoticed*, but the word is also used to
indicate the exploits of a club, usually provincial, who
are not getting the *credit they deserve*: 'Norwich's
charge up the table has gone largely *unnoticed* outside
of Norfolk'.

Unsettled: Standard epithet for players who are
likely to or have already put in a transfer request.
Usually their stated grievance is a *lack of **first-team
football***.

Unveil: Your new **signing** will always be *unveiled* at
a press conference. Perhaps the metaphor dates back
to a time when the announcement of a new signing
came as a surprise. Now that media coverage is so sat-
urated, the veil is almost always translucent.

Unwanted: Can denote a player who is *out of **favour***
but more usually combined with *tag* or *nickname*:
'Southgate carries with him the *unwanted* tag of the
man who missed the penalty'. When teams face some
record-breaking ignominy – the first Premiership
team to lose to non-league opposition, or the club
to score fewest goals in a season – this *unwanted*
achievement should be referred to as a *dubious hon-
our*.

Up and down: 'Kieron Dyer gets *up and down* very well'. A locution referring not to a player's trampolining talents nor to prowess of any other sort, but to his ability to move swiftly from one end of the pitch to another, *box to box*. Such a player tends to have a good *engine*. In another sense, a good *up and down* does not in football refer to a neat chip and putt to escape with par, but a situation where a *dead-ball specialist shapes* the ball over the wall and under the bar.

Upend: The verb is a *no-nonsense* way of saying *to foul*. Often leads to an *undisputed penalty*.

Utility player: A footballer whose versatility goes some way to compensate for a lack of ability. Or, perhaps more cruelly, a player supposedly good at everything but actually good at nothing. Often there is a faint hint that the player concerned does *anything asked of him* because he does not have the skill to *hold down* a regular position. Perhaps strengthened by usage in World War II when the word 'utility' stamped on consumer goods ensured no unnecessary extravagance. There may be brilliant *utility players*, *equally at home* in defence or midfield (some of the Dutch *total footballers* come to mind) but they are spared this adjective which, as in 'utility room', describes something not only utilitarian but modest, perfunctory, to the point of being ignored.

V

Varsity Clash: Cambridge United v Oxford United. But their fans are about as likely to refer to the game in this way, as the students are to go to it. One of those terms, like **Battle of Britain**, wished upon football supporters by journalists.

Vintage: A slight upgrade on **trademark**. Add the player's first name for extra effect: 'That run and shot was absolutely *vintage* Michael Owen'. Or another way of putting it, from the restaurant rather than the wine cellar: 'That was a Michel Platini *special*'.

Virtual spectator: 'Preud'homme was a *virtual spectator* for the last twenty minutes'. This is how the goalkeeper on the dominant (usually winning) side should be described, the converse of the phrase **busier of the keepers**. Although such keepers may actually have done nothing but watch the game, the *virtual* is necessary, lest you think the keeper went and sat in one of the stands to do his watching. It is incidentally unheard of to describe a football supporter as a 'spectator'.

Vision: Rather like **awareness**, but this noun pays more extravagant tribute to the ability of the player who has it. The noun does not always require an adjective (though players may be vouchsafed with *great vision*). Nor should you specify of what the player has *vision*. It is implicitly understood if you say 'Metgod has *vision*' or 'Metgod's *vision* is brilliant' that this is *vision* of team-mates whom he can bring into play with a *defence-splitting* pass, and nothing to do with his futuristic, utopian conceptualisations – or not necessarily: you never know with these intellectual foreign players.

Visit: In an attempt to assign a gentlemanly quality to a fixture, this noun is substituted for **clash** or **encounter**. Used before and rarely after a game: 'County will be unchanged for the *visit* of Rovers'. Similarly the plural noun *visitors* is used to denote the opposition or away team, almost exclusively in polite programme notes and on non-league scoreboards, but occasionally also in press reports as a method of avoiding repetition of the away team's name. Never uttered by fans, be they the **home faithful** or the **travelling army**.

W

Wage-bill: 'Despite a hefty increase on last year's *wage-bill*, Arsenal's still looks miserly compared with Manchester United's'. In football there does not seem to be such a thing as a 'payroll'; instead there is always a *wage-bill* which tends to *spiral out of control*.

Wake-up call: What superior teams may receive early in a game or season to ensure *complacency* does not *creep in*: 'The defeat at Chelsea was a real *wake-up call* and the boys have strung together some good results since then'. If it turns out the *wake-up call* is the presage of worse to come then it will have been a *rude awakening*.

Walk: 'Leworthy really had to *walk* for that one'. Said of players who get their **marching orders** and can *have no complaints*. Perhaps it's because they will tend to trudge off the pitch more slowly than players being substituted. Or perhaps we are to understand that such players are *walking the plank*. At all events, it can be a *long* or *lonely* walk back to the dressing room. By contrast, if a team is having *a walk* or *a stroll in the park*, they are definitely in the **comfort zone**. A close cousin of **exhibition stuff**.

Waltz: 'McCarthy just *waltzed* past Drury there'. Perhaps because of their *dancing feet* or *twinkle toes*, this verb seems to be used primarily of wingers who are giving their full-backs a **torrid time**.

Want-away: Tabloid adjective for an **unsettled** player: '*Want-away* striker Frank Worthington *slapped in* another transfer request yesterday'. You never see: 'Frank Worthington, the striker who wants to leave Leicester…'.

Watched: *Well watched* is the expression if a goal-keeper or defender **deals with** a ball into the **mix** by not actually playing the ball. Almost a reflex in these circumstances, but sometimes used with heavy irony: 'Let's just say that was *well watched* by Geoff Crudgington'.

Wave away: 'Appeals for a penalty were *waved away* by Martin Bodenham'. Describes the refusal of the referee to give a decision, even if he makes no hand signals at all, just as he can be said to *point to the spot* without actually pointing. The reported action has become such a proxy for a refusal to give a penalty decision that you do not even need to refer to appeals: 'Branch *tumbled* under a De Vos challenge and it looked a penalty – but referee Eddie Evans *waved it away*'.

Way: Rather pompously, a club can convince itself that it has a certain copyrighted style of play or code of ethics: 'Just lumping the ball upfield is not the Tottenham *way*'; 'Not pulling together for each other is just not the MK Dons *way*'. Coaching staff can congratulate themselves on methods purportedly unique to themselves: 'We've *certain ways* of *doing things* here at Hednesford Town **Football Club** and the players have to fit into that'. See also **all about**.

Wealth of experience: *Beleaguered* managers will announce a new *signing* in their programme notes with the phrase 'he brings with him a *wealth of experience* to the *football club*'. Such players are, of course, affordable veterans past their prime.

Wednesday night in Rochdale: The location is usually northern, the date invariably midweek for the emblematic, hypothetical fixture that a good player of suspect temperament (usually foreign) is unlikely to relish and will want to shirk. Often found in interrogative form: 'Passing it about on this stage is all very well, but can he do it on *a Tuesday night in Grimsby*?' The sobering rhetorical question is designed to check runaway enthusiasm for a superstar.

Week in week out: A phrase used to denote consistency, or the lack of it: 'Gough performs *week in week out* and is a great example to the younger players'; 'We did well tonight but we have to string these performances together *week in week out*'. If surveying a whole career you can enlarge the scope to *year in year out*, and see *tracksuit manager* for an example of *day in day out* involvement. There is a related expression to chide a player for not doing something expected of him: 'Dublin should be winning the *aerial* challenges with Forssell *every day of the week*'.

Week's wages: The unit of measure for club fines, even if this usually gives no indication of the quantum of the penalty: 'Collymore was fined *two weeks' wages* for his latest indiscretion at La Manga'. When the wages are counted out (say, just for example, in *The Daily Mail*), cue indignation at players' vast stipends.

Weight: Can be used of a pass, often *perfectly weighted*. But like players ('Gascoigne is not his *ideal* *weight'*), passes tend not to be described as 'over-weight'. The *weight* or *burden of expectation* is what new managers or players at *a club as big as this* have to *deal with*.

Welcome: As well as being a useful alternative to *versus* when reading out a cup draw on the radio – 'Barnsley *welcome* Plymouth Argyle' – the noun can appear euphemistically in managers' programme notes to incite booing of former *crowd favourites*: 'Hassan Kachloul was a *legend* here at Southampton and I'm sure you'll be giving him a *warm welcome* tonight'. Similarly, commentators enjoy greeting a particularly *robust* tackle which leaves a *debutant* (usually a *fancy* foreign player) in the English game groaning, with the cheerfully ironic words: '*Welcome* to the *Premiership*, Juan Sebastian!'

Well-documented: Euphemistic phrase to describe a matter that has been *all over the papers*. Often reserved for a managerial departure or the personal problems of a player: 'What happened at QPR has been *well documented*, and for the moment I'm concentrating on my media commitments'. Despite the documentation, the individual concerned, especially if he is Paul Merson, often then proceeds to talk about things again.

Wembley: There was a time when the world knew only two *twin towers*. Now there are four and yet none. *Wembley*, like the World Trade Center, is no longer. Comparisons end there. *Wembley* had always been a destination more imagined and hoped for than it was experienced and arrived at by most fans (hence *the road to Wembley* and *Wembley way*, set phrases which added to the mystique of the FA Cup as a sort of Holy Grail). Yet its destruction has left a void in the language of football. The special *energy-sapping* properties of its turf cannot be found in Cardiff or at any other grounds. While *Wembley* was there, it seemed easier to believe that a supernatural force, against the odds and beyond rational comprehension, was impelling you because your *name was on the Cup.* And, now that it has been razed, the fatalistic cup song – '*Que Serà Serà*, whatever will be will be' – languishes without a rhyme.

Wheel away: The action of a scorer in the immediate aftermath of scoring. At such moments the *wheeling away* is performed in *celebration, delight* or *triumph*. Very commonly seen in the captions to photographs in programmes or newspapers, taken just after the ball has hit *the back of the net.* Not to be confused with *reel away*, which players sometimes do, **theatrically**, if there has been the *suspicion* of a headbutt.

Wheeling and dealing: What **cash-strapped** managers are always required to do: 'Given the *resources* at this club I'm going to have to do some *wheeling and dealing* in the transfer market'.

Whistler: Thesaurus-driven alternative to *referee*: 'The Melton Mowbray *whistler* was **spot on** five minutes later…' *Arbiter* is another option driven by a similar desire not to repeat yourself.

White line: 'We respect France but once we step over *that white line* in Portugal all that will go *out of the window*'; 'He's a lovely lad but sometimes, when he gets over *that white line* on a Saturday afternoon, the red mist descends'. Football people specifically call to mind the markings on the perimeter of the pitch when they want to emphasise that they are crossing a threshold.

Width: A footballing elixir, possessed by all effective *attacking units*. Teams that *lack width* really ought to go out and buy a *winger* or two. But *width* does not just mean **wingers**. The abstraction seems to be used all the more since the advent of wing-backs in the modern game, who *augment* the attack by *providing width*.

Will: Peter Jones, the lamented radio commentator of the 1970s and 1980s, liked a future tense when describing a match in real time: 'Case *will* find Heighway, who *will* pass back to Callaghan, who *will* …'. Perhaps this mannerism served to disguise the fact that, like all radio commentators, he was always a little behind play, or perhaps it lent to the passing moves he so evocatively described an aura of synergetic inevitability.

Wily: Often combined with *old campaigner*. Can be used of a **midfield general** or an experienced centre-half (particularly if he is South American and playing in Italy), but also of managers either for the way they motivate players or for their **wheeling and dealing**.

Win: The noun is interchangeable with *victory*, except faintly nationalistic hues may surface in the latter case: 'England are now *in the driving-seat* in group D, after their *heroic victory* over Turkey'. A *win* is less likely to be glorious, as in the truism that *a win is a win*, and managers celebrate *coming away* or *getting away* with a *win* of any kind, even if it is **ugly** or *not* **pretty**. In radio commentaries the verb is used much less obtrusively to indicate the capture of possession, particularly in *aerial* **battles**: 'Phil Chapple has *won* so much in the air tonight'. Whereas a *ball-winner* tends to win the ball on the **deck**.

Wingers: If beating their man, *wingers* tend to be *tricky, difficult*; if not, they may be described as *mercurial, enigmatic, frustrating*. Since 4-4-2 replaced 2-3-5, *wide man* is now threatening to supersede *winger* as the generic term (see also **width** for 3-5-2).

Winner: The decisive or deciding goal. Football reporters tend to be careful, perhaps a bit ponderous, in indicating that you do not know that a goal is a *winner* until the end of the match. Thus: 'On 35 minutes, Iwelumo hit what turned out to be the *winner*'. The verbs to *turn out* or to *prove* ensure retrospective precision in these cases.

Wire: What title races go *right down to*. An extension of the **horse race** metaphor, even if American in origin.

Withdraw: Strikers may be described as *withdrawn* or playing in a *withdrawn role*. This denotes the act of dropping *deep* rather than introspection of any kind. When managers *withdraw a player* to make a substitution (rather than *removing* the player or *taking him off* the pitch) this more temperate verb may help to give the impression that the manager is thinking *tactically*.

Wives and girlfriends: Progressive managers will allow the players away on international **duty** a day or two with *wives and girlfriends*. The language of football has not got round to calling them anything else, maybe because **partners** is a term which is already taken.

Wobble: A verb employed at moments when a team likely to win the competition suffers an unexpected setback: 'Arsenal had a little *wobble* at the Reebok, but still should be good enough to clinch the title'. *Wobbler* is a variant usage.

Wonderkid: Or *boy wonder*. An exceptional *product* of a team's *youth policy*. Sometimes translated back into its German antecedent *Wunderkind*.

Woodwork: The accepted noun for the description of post and/or crossbar, even though the frames of the goal are no longer wooden: 'It was just not Darlington's day. The Quakers hit the *woodwork* yet again ten minutes from time.' Less specific but also less ambiguous than saying 'the Quakers hit the bar again...'.

Words: *Harsh* or *choice* ones can be *said* or *had* at half-time; *heated* ones in the tunnel (whereas the euphemistic **pleasantries** tend to be exchanged on the pitch or in front of the **dugouts**). Strangely, referees *have a word*, usually a *quiet* one, rather than *words*. *Talks* are more reserved for transfer negotiations: they are *opened* with a player, often *stall* or are *put on hold*, and then are *completed*.

Work-rate: A comparatively recent term, its pseudo-scientific flavour suited to a generation weaned on Carling Opta statistics and Fantasy Football points. It really means *effort* and *application* but perhaps something more too, like a willingness to chase **lost causes** (as in 'Savage's *work-rate* was phenomenal') which, in football, is a virtue: 'We've got to match them for *work-rate*, if we're going to get anything out of the game'. See also **industry.**

Wraps: What new signings or, more occasionally, new tactics, are kept under. Similar ideas are treating a youngster with *kid gloves* and wrapping your more fragile stars in *cotton wool*.

X

X-rated: Censorious certification of tackles which are *over the top* in every sense, or of games where there have been many such tackles: 'Once referee Riley lost his grip on proceedings, the game descended into *real x-rated stuff*'. There are no other gradations of rating, like PG or 18, in football parlance.

Y

Yard: Standard imperial unit of measure for *pace*. Some players are unfortunate to *lack* a *yard* of pace to begin with, others *lose* it as they get older. In the plural, used to indicate how far a forward has strayed past the *last man*, especially in *situations* where the linesman does not raise his flag and said player is *controversially ruled onside*: 'Butragueño looked *yards* offside there but was allowed to go on'. *A mile* is the alternative to *yards* in this context.

Ye: The archaic second-person form can yet be heard on two occasions in Britain. On Sundays: '*Ye* Holy Angels Bright…'; on Saturdays: 'Come on *ye* Blu-ues'. *You* can now be used in its stead, in both cases.

Yellow card: The footballing equivalent to walking on eggs, players are always described as being *on a yellow card* in the course of a match or particularly during a tournament when bookings can add up to a suspension.

Your: 'Your Klinsmanns, your Stoichkovs…' The second-person possessive allied to a plural guarantees the sententious force of this phrase. The plural has the paradoxical effect of pointing up the uniqueness of the player: 'To compete with *your* Zidanes, *your* Henrys, you have to be a bit special'. See also *the **likes of***.

Youth policy: Always seems to be *progressive* or *forward-looking*, and bears fruit in the shape of *products of the youth scheme* or *youth products*. When it works superlatively well, you may talk of a *production line of talent*. The League Cup now exists chiefly to give the managers of big clubs a chance to *blood* youngsters.

Yo-yo: Once fashionable term to describe the *effect* whereby a *yo-yo team* moves up and down between two divisions, too good for one and too poor for the other. Sheffield Wednesday were the *yo-yo team* of the 1950s, probably in the heyday of the *yo-yo*, which has fended off more modern counterparts to describe the recent exploits of Leicester City, who are ***many people's idea*** of the latest *yo-yo team*. A connected joke is the description of Walsall as champions of the old Division Four or Lecce as champions of Serie B *every other year*.

Z

Z: *Row Z* is a long way from the pitch and so, by inference, the hypothetical destination of any ***no-nonsense*** clearance. Defenders who put *safety first* by playing *within their limitations* can be praised, but a reference to the back of the stand may also depict a badly over-

hit pass: 'He tried to find Fredgaard on the other
wing, but that's gone straight into *Row Z*'. Old-
school managers may even condone their players putting the opposition into the stands along with the
ball: 'County boss Billy Dearden was left fuming:
"O'Driscoll should have finished in *Row Z* but we
were too nice"'.